Sustainable Growth in the African Economy

The current growth path in sub-Saharan Africa is not following the Lewis model where labour moves from low-productivity agriculture to higher productivity manufacturing. Instead, it is moving directly to inappropriate (import and labour-saving) methods. This book seeks to show how this distorted growth process leaves out the major resource of these countries – labour – and ends up creating unstable employment and underemployment, leading to inequality and poverty. In this way it demonstrates how the entire growth process may be rendered unstable and unsustainable.

Sustainable Growth in the African Economy considers whether the relatively rapid growth of recent years can be maintained or improved upon, with a focus on the process of industrialisation. Basing itself on a well-known dual-economy model, the proposed book focuses on several major problems of industrialisation, which has long been seen as the means of structural change in an economy which begins from a low income level. The book considers how the future trajectory of sub-Saharan Africa compares to recent success stories on other continents, and explains how factors such as rapid population growth and capital and import-intensive technology in manufacturing could foreshadow future social and political problems.

This book will be essential reading to students and policymakers who are concerned with the existing pattern of African growth.

Jeffrey James is Emeritus Professor of Development Economics at Tilburg University, the Netherlands.

Routledge Studies in Development Economics

Sustainable Growth in the African Economy
How Durable is Africa's Recent Performance?

Jeffrey James

Routledge
Taylor & Francis Group

LONDON AND NEW YORK

First published 2017
by Routledge

2 Park Square, Milton Park, Abingdon, Oxfordshire OX14 4RN
52 Vanderbilt Avenue, New York, NY 10017

Routledge is an imprint of the Taylor & Francis Group, an informa business

First issued in paperback 2019

British Library Cataloguing in Publication Data
A catalogue record for this book is available from the British Library

Library of Congress Cataloging in Publication Data
Names: James, Jeffrey, 1949- author.
Title: Sustainable growth in the African economy : how durable is Africa's
recent performance? / Jeffrey James.
Description: Abingdon, Oxon ; New York, NY : Routledge, 2017. |
Includes bibliographical references and index.
Identifiers: LCCN 2016047489| ISBN 9781138648586 (hardback) |
ISBN 9781315626321 (ebook)
Subjects: LCSH: Economic development—Africa. | Africa—Economic
policy. | Africa—Economic conditions—21st century.
Classification: LCC HC800 .J3625 2017 | DDC 338.96/07—dc23
LC record available at https://lccn.loc.gov/2016047489

ISBN: 978-1-138-64858-6 (hbk)
ISBN: 978-0-367-87778-1 (pbk)

Typeset in Bembo
by diacriTech, Chennai

Contents

Figures

Tables

Acknowledgements

Throughout the process of writing this book, I was greatly helped by my editors Emily Kindleysides and Elanor Best. They have been friendly, encouraging and efficient.

During the production and editing of the typescript I am indebted to a number of people at Tilburg University, especially Ailsa Rainer. Also generous of their time and patience have been Kristina Melicherova, Nicole van de Ven and Mirjam Pennings.

Finally, I would like to express my sincere thanks to Professors Fiona Tregenna and Margaret McMillan for permission to use material from their unpublished work.

Chapter 8 is from Jeffrey James (2014), 'Is there a renewed role for appropriate technology in the new global innovation system?', *Journal of International Development*, doi:10.1002/jid.2986, by permission of Wiley.

Chapter 9 is from Jeffrey James (2000), 'Trait-making for labour-intensive technology in Sub-Saharan Africa', *Research Policy* 29,6:757–766, by permission of Elsevier.

Chapter 10 is from Jeffrey James (2006), 'An institutional critique of recent attempts to measure technological capabilities across countries', *Journal of Economic Issues*, 40, 3:743–766, by permission of Taylor & Francis.

Table 1.1 is from World Bank, (2015b), 'The Global Economy in Transition', *Global Economic Prospects*, Washington, DC: World Bank, doi: 10.1596/978-1-4648-0483-0, License: Creative Commons Attribution CC BY 3.0 IGO.

Tables 2.2, 2.3, Figure 2.1 and Appendix Table 1, Chapter 2, are from UNIDO and UNCTAD, *The Economic Development of Africa Report*, 2011, by permission of UNIDO and UNCTAD. Tables 2.4 and 2.7 are from Dinh, H.; Palmade, Vincent; Chandra, Vandana; Cassar, Frances. 2012, *Light Manufacturing in Africa: Targeted Policies to Enhance Private Investment and Create Jobs*, Washington, DC: Africa Development Forum, World Bank. https://openknowledge.worldbank.org/handle/10986/2245. License: CC BY 3.0.IGO.

Table 2.5 is from World Bank (2012), World Development Report 2013: Jobs, World Development Report, Washington DC ©World Bank. https://openknowledge.worldbank.org/handle/10986/11843. License: CC BY 3.0 IGO.

Table 2.6 is from Golub, S. & Hayat, F. (2014), 'Employment, unemployment and underemployment in Africa; Wider Working paper series, no. 14. This table is reproduced by permission of UNU-WIDER, Helsinki, which commissioned the original research and holds copyright thereon.

Figures 3.1, 3.3, 3.4, 3.5 and 3.6 are from Fig. 1 in Lewis, W.A. (1954), 'Economic development with unlimited supplies of labour', *The Manchester School, 2.2*, 2:139–191, with permission of Wiley. Tables 3.1, 3.2 and 3.3 are from World Population Prospects, 2015 revision, Economic & Social Affairs, ©2015 United Nations. Reprinted with the permission of the United Nations.

Table 4.3 is from World Bank (2011), World Development Report 2011: Conflict, Security and Development. World Bank. ©World Bank, https://openknowledge. worldbank.org/handle10986/4389. License: CC BY 3.0 IGO.

Table 4.4 is from UNODC (2011), Global Homicide Report, with the permission of UNODC.

Table 5.1 is from Tregenna, F. (2012), 'Sectoral labour-intensity in South Africa', NEDLAC Labour-Intensity Report, unpublished paper, with the permission of the author.

Table 5.2 is from United Nations Economic Commission for Africa (UNECA), Dynamic Industrial Policy in Africa: Innovative Institutions, Effective Processes and Flexible Mechanisms, ©United Nations Economic Commission for Africa, 2014, with permission of UNECA.

Table 5.3 is from Dinh, H; Palmade, Vincent; Chandra, Vandana; Cassar, Frances (2012), Light Manufacturing in Africa: Targeted Policies to Enhance Private Investment & Create Jobs. African Development Forum. World Bank. ©World Bank. https://openknowledge.worldbank.org/handle/10986/2245. Licence: CC BY 3.0 IGO.

Table 5.4 is from Farole, Thomas (2011), Special Economic Zones in Africa: Comparing Performance and Learning from Global Experience, Directions in Development: Trade. World Bank. ©World Bank. https://openknowledge.worldbank .org/handle/10986/2268. License: CC BY IGO.

Tables 5.5 and 5.6 are from Pack, H. (1982), 'Aggregate implications of factor substitution in industrial processes', *Journal of Development Economics, 11*,1:1–38 with permission of Elsevier.

Table 5.7 is from Lecraw, D. (1977), 'Direct Investment by firms from less developed countries', *Oxford Economic Papers*, 29,3:442–457, with permission from Oxford University Press.

Table 6.1 is from Pigato, M. and Tang, W. (2015), China and Africa: Expanding Economic Ties in an Evolving Global Context, World Bank, Washington DC ©World Bank. https://openknowledge.worldbank.org/handle/10986/21788. License: CC BY 3.0 IGO.

Table 6.2 is from Edwards, L. and Jenkins, R. (2013), 'The impact of Chinese import penetration on the South African manufacturing sector', Southern Africa Labour and Development Research Unit, Working Paper no. 102. Cape Town: SALDRU, University of Cape Town, with permission of the authors.

Table 6.3 is from Ozawa, T. (2015), 'Next great industrial transmigration: relocating China's factories to sub-Saharan Africa, flying-geese style', *Asia-Pacific Economic Cooperation*, Columbia University, with permission from APEC and the author.

Figures 6.1 and 6.2 are from Lancaster, K. (1996), 'A new approach to consumer theory', *Journal of Political Economy*, 74, 2:132–157, with permission of University of Chicago Press.

Table 7.1 is from Ghani, E. and O'Connell, S. (2014), 'Can Service Be a Growth Escalator in Low Income Countries?' Policy Research Working Paper; No. 6971. World Bank Group, Washington, D.C. ©World Bank. https://openknowledg. worldbank.org/handle/10986/19352. License: CC BY 3.0 IGO.

Table 7.2 is from Martins, P. (2014), Structural change in Ethiopia: an employment perspective, Policy research working paper, no. 6749, World Bank, Washington, DC ©World Bank. https://openknowledge.worldbank.org/handle/10986/16829. License: CC BY 3.0 IGO.

Figure 8.2 is from James, J. and Stewart, F. (1981), 'New products: a discussion of the welfare effects of the introduction of new products in developing countries', *Oxford Economic Papers*, 33,1:81–107, with permission of Oxford University Press.

Figures 9.A1 and 9.A2 are from James, J. (1999), 'Trait-taking versus trait-making in technical choice: the case of Africa', *Journal of International Development*, 11,6: 797–810, with permission of Wiley.

Table 10.1 is from Nasir, A. Ali, T. Shahdin, S. and Rahman, T. (2011), 'Technology achievement index 2009: ranking and comparative study of nations,' *Scientometrics*, 87:41–62, with permission of Springer.

Table 10.2 is from Chinapah, V. (2003), 'Monitoring learning achievement (MLA) in Africa', Association for the Development of Education in Africa, ADEA biennial meeting, Mauritius, with permission of the author.

Table 10.3 is from the UNDP, *Human Development Report*, 2001.

1   Introduction

Almost thirty years ago Bloom and Freeman observed that:

> The economies of the less developed countries are about to face perhaps the greatest challenge in their histories: generating a sufficient number of jobs at reasonable wages to absorb their rapidly growing populations into productive employment. In terms of absolute magnitude, this challenge has no precedent in human history.
>
> (Bloom & Freeman, 1987:106)

The main goal of this book is to assess how well Africa (henceforth to be understood as sub-Saharan Africa) has responded – and will respond in the future – to the challenge described in the above quotation. Briefly summarised, the argument is that the growth trajectory of African countries has not – since 1995 – followed the main tenets of the dual-economy model as espoused originally by Lewis (1954). That is, instead of labour moving from agriculture to manufacturing as the model posits, large numbers of workers have remained instead in the vast informal sector, earning low wages in unproductive jobs. Much of the reason for this, I contend, has to do with the choice of a highly capital-intensive development strategy and the eschewal of the alternative labour-using model employed successfully in parts of Asia. The book seeks to show that this process neglects the major resource of African countries – namely, labour[1] – and ends up creating major problems of un(der)employment, inequality and poverty, which may, over time, make the entire growth process unstable and unsustainable.

It is not that there has been no structural change. On the contrary, the share of agriculture in the total output has fallen in many African countries since 1995 and some of those previously in the sector have taken up more productive jobs in formal services. The problem is rather that the share of manufacturing has gone down on average as a percentage of total output and aggregate exports (see next chapter).[2] Moreover, the share of labour-intensive, low-technology products in manufacturing has also decreased. And by no means least, the choice of technology within light manufacturing has often been capital- and import-intensive, rather than intensive in labour and reliant on local inputs (James, 1995).[3]

So, while Chapter 3 shows that the Lewis model appears to work well as an explanation of what happened in the now developed and certain developing

Asian countries, it has not fared very well at all in Africa. Some of the reasons for this have been explored by Lewis himself, twenty-five years after the publication of his original paper in 1954. In 1979, that is, in answering the question of whether the modern sector will grow fast enough to absorb 'those who wish to leave the traditional sector' (1979:221), he recognised the problems created by the small relative size of the former sector, the 'pervasiveness of labour-saving innovations' (1979:221) and the rapid growth of the labour force.

Of these, probably the least well known is the small initial size of the formal sector in Africa. The point is actually a simple, arithmetic one, though it has profound implications for the ease with which structural change can occur. Consider, by way of example, two countries that are identical in all respects other than the relative size of their formal sectors. Each economy has a working-age population of 50 million people and an annual increase in the labour supply of 1 million. In the one economy, however, the initial size of the formal sector is 4 million (or 8 per cent of the total) and in the other it is 8 million (or 16 per cent of the total). Just to absorb the increase in the labour force, the first-mentioned economy has to grow by 25 per cent, as opposed to the figure of 'only' 12.5 per cent in the latter, where the formal sector is twice as large.

To even begin absorbing labour from the informal sector, moreover, these growth rates will need to be even higher. Unfortunately for the working of the Lewis model in Africa, evidence from the next chapter shows that the informal sector is above 80 per cent, and in many cases above 90 per cent, in a selected sample of countries from the region. Given an average population growth of around 2.6 per cent per annum, the demand for labour requirement becomes excessive as shown in Chapter 4, especially when it is combined with the tendency towards capital intensity described in the following chapter.

In spite of these problems, however, African growth over the past fifteen years has been of the order of 5 per cent per annum, a rate that is high by international standards, even though it was generated from a very low base in most cases. Indeed, so much did this performance exceed what went before it, that there has been much talk of an African 'miracle'. In the next section, I question whether such talk is justified.

Has there been an African growth 'miracle'?

One may call it a miracle that the commodity boom in Africa has lasted as long as it has. After all, it is this that has driven a good deal of the growth in total output since 2000 (Dinh et al., 2012). In a more serious vein, however, there is a good reason not to wax too lyrically over the recorded growth in total output. For, it is true, by definition, that what matters to individual welfare is *not* total growth, but rather growth in *per capita* terms. And in these terms, Africa's performance has been much less impressive than the total output figures that give rise to talk about miracles.

Consider in this regard, the entries shown in Table 1.1.

The entries in the table are obtained by subtracting from the total growth rate, the rate of population growth, which in Africa has been of the order of

Table 1.1 Per capita growth rates in Africa and Asia 2000–2017 (%)

Region	2000–10	2011	2012	2013	2014	2015	2016	2017
Africa (sub-Sahara)	3.1	1.7	1.6	2.4	2.1	1.7	2.1	2.5
South Asia	5.1	5.5	3.9	4.8	5.5	5.7	6.0	6.2
East Asia & the Pacific	8.2	7.6	6.7	6.5	6.2	6.1	6.1	6.1

Source: World Bank, 2015b.

2.6 per cent per annum, higher than in any other region of the world. The adjusted per capita rates for Africa are modest and well below those for South and East Asia. In this sense, it would be more appropriate to talk of a South Asian than an African miracle. Note, further, that it is the per capita figures that influence poverty and the modest improvements in Africa shown in Table 1.1 help to explain why the numbers of poor in this region have grown since 1995, even though poverty rates have declined.

I would suggest, therefore, that it is as yet inappropriate to speak of growth miracles in Africa, except in the limited sense of a comparison with what occurred in the 1970s and 1980s (when growth rates were abysmally low).

In defence of a dual-economy approach to growth

It might be thought by some that the Lewis framework, as set out in 1954 and revisited in 1979, has become outdated as a means of analysing contemporary African development. Yet, as I now try to show, there are good reasons for retaining the basic framework of the model, even though certain amendments to it need to be made. Indeed, it is by focusing on these limitations that *one can better understand what needs to be done in order to promote more rapid growth in the region.*

Consider, to begin with, that the framework in question makes much of the inter-sectoral difference in productivity in developing countries. Consider further that the evidence available tends to suggest that such differences are especially pronounced in Africa. Page (2012), for example, has studied differences in productivity across nine sectors in a sample of developed and developing countries. What he finds is that

> whether measured by the ratio of the highest to the lowest sectoral labour-productivity or by the coefficient of variation of (the log of) sectoral labour productivity, the differences are least for the high-income countries and greatest for Africa. The variation among sectors in Africa is particularly large: the average ratio of highest to lowest productivity sectors in Africa exceeds that for Latin America and Asia by more than 2 to 1.
>
> (Page, 2012:88–89)

More recently, Golub and Hayat (2014) have also lent their support to the dual-economy model. At one point, for example, they claim,

> The celebrated Lewis (1954) model still provides the starting point for understanding African dualism as resulting from low demand for labour in the modern sector. The model features a large traditional sector with subsistence incomes and a small modern sector paying much higher wages. The process of economic development involves expansion of the modern (formal) sector through capital accumulation, gradually absorbing surplus labour from the subsistence (informal) sector.
>
> (Golub & Hayat, 2014:6)

At another point, these authors claim that the Lewis model currently has more relevance to African growth than it did at the time when it was first published. Thus,

> At the time of writing his classic article, Arthur Lewis (1954) noted that much of Africa did not fully fit his model… However, due to rapid population growth combined with limited development of the formal sector, Lewis's framework now fits very well for much of low-income Africa, dominated by subsistence agriculture and small-scale family firms.
>
> (Golub & Hayat, 2014:5)

The most compelling case for a dualistic approach to growth, however, has been made by Rodrik (2013). He usefully distinguishes between two 'traditions' in growth economics. One of them is based on neoclassical growth theory, as first promulgated by Solow (1956), and the other is the dual-economy approach that has just been described. The former emphasises growth 'fundamentals', such as skills, instructions and geography, which, in concert, help to determine long-run income levels. Yet, despite undeniable improvements in many fundamentals (such as political institutions and economic liberalisation), African growth has yet to achieve anything like the rates achieved historically by the now developed countries and some emerging Asian nations such as Vietnam. The problem, as Rodrik sees it, is that

> while the region's fundamentals have improved, the payoffs to macroeconomic stability and improved governance are mainly to foster resilience and lay the groundwork for growth, rather than to generate productivity on their own.
>
> (Rodrik, 2014:1)

This is where the complementary need for a structural change perspective asserts itself.

The point is that although contemporary growth economics has forced this earlier tradition somewhat into the background,

> it is clear that the heterogeneity in productive structures which dual-economy models capture continue to have great relevance to low-income economies

such as those in Sub-Saharan Africa. A hallmark of developing countries is the wide dispersion in productivity across economic activities – modern versus traditional, formal versus informal, traded versus non-traded ... and even within individual sectors.

(Rodrik, 2014:5)

What is especially telling, though, is Rodrik's recent finding that reinforces a dualistic perspective. In particular, he has found that 'modern, organized manufacturing industries *are* different: they do exhibit *unconditional* convergence, unlike the rest of the economy' (Rodrik 2014:16). This, he regards as a

rather remarkable result. It says that modern manufacturing industries converge to the global productivity frontier regardless of geographical disadvantages, lousy institutions, or bad policies...what is striking is the presence of convergence, in at least certain parts of the economy, even in the absence of good fundamentals.

(Rodrik, 2014:6, emphasis in original)

Yet, formal sector manufacturing, to which the theory of unconditional convergence applies, has been languishing in Africa: employment in such firms in Ethiopia and Senegal, for example, is only 6 per cent of overall manufacturing employment. Thus it is that Rodrik (2014) sees a marked difference between structural change that has occurred in Africa with what took place in early European countries and their Asian followers. In both cases,

labor is moving out of agriculture and rural areas. But formal manufacturing industries are not the main beneficiary. Urban migrants are being absorbed largely into services that are not particularly productive and into informal activities. The pace of industrialization is much too slow, for the convergence dynamics to play out in full force.

(Rodrik, 2014:9)

Part of the reason why formal manufacturing consists of so small a proportion of the total employment in the sector in Africa has to do with technology (as argued in Chapter 3). For one thing, there are choices to be made out of manufacturing branches which differ – sometimes widely – in their labour intensity (textiles, say, versus machinery production). Then there are choices between alternatives *within* the selected branches. The pattern of modern technical change is such that the range of choice at any time is itself determined by where the new technologies are generated. Since this takes place mainly in countries which are increasingly capital-abundant and labour scarce, the range of options moves in a continuously labour-saving direction. In this regard, Pack (1982) has convincingly demonstrated that much extra employment could be gained in a typical African country, if the most labour-saving alternatives were rejected in favour of relatively efficient, labour-intensive methods in manufacturing.

None of this is to say, however, that the study of structural change in Africa needs to be confined to the manufacturing sector. The formal sector, as Lewis (1979) points out, also contains certain service activities which are relatively productive and in some cases tradeable. New digital technologies, for example, are changing the possibilities that are available in this sector (e.g., by outsourcing of business services). The question that needs to be addressed, therefore, is whether structural change in Africa can be based on these emerging activities rather than – or in addition to – more familiar processes in manufacturing. This issue is taken up in Chapter 7.

Technology

Also emphasised below are crucial technological issues related to the manufacturing sector. I shall argue that failures in these areas have been less about active policy mistakes than they have been about near-total policy *neglect*.

During the import-substitution phase of the 1970s and 1980s, for example, decision-makers were more intent on initiating large-scale, foreign-financed projects than in examining the efficacy of the technology that was typically selected by Western aid donors and consultants (James, 1995). Any chance to build up a local climate where technology and technological capabilities were emphasised went sorely unmet. Later, during the period of structural adjustment in African industry, the same result was obtained, because the neoclassical model underlying the new policies was no more attuned to the need for building up domestic capabilities (to use and adapt foreign methods of production) than it was in the import-substitution phase. Again, many years that could have been expended on a more technological approach to manufacturing went missed.

Yet, as Lall (2005) and others have convincingly argued, the acquisition of adequate domestic technological capabilities is nothing less than essential for industrial success. This:

> requires more than a good investment climate – it needs the ability to respond vigorously in an increasingly competitive and technology-oriented environment. This ability *does not arise automatically*. It is based on cumulative effort to build a range of technological, managerial and institutional capabilities: just opening up to global markets, technology and capital flows, without a base of capabilities, means that economies cannot competitively handle new industrial technologies. If they cannot, they risk marginalisation in a globally integrated market.
>
> (Lall, 2005, 15:2, emphasis added)

It would be interesting and useful in this regard if there existed a conceptually sound index of technology capabilities that could be used to compare different countries and to track changes in a single country over time. But though there are measures that purport to capture capabilities, they tend to be based on the ability to *create* new products and processes rather than to *adapt* to innovations, which is so crucial to African industries (see Chapter 10). Moreover, these indices tend to change rather quickly over time, thus making it difficult to track a given country's progress over time. An index designed specifically for Africa needs to be formulated, as argued below.

Other technological issues, however, do receive extended treatment in the chapters that follow. Chapter 3, for example, addresses the issue of technical change and how its directional bias skews the demand for labour in the Lewis model. Relatedly, in Chapter 6, I discuss the implications of an emerging global system, in which innovation (and foreign investment) take place in emerging countries such as India and China as well as in the already developed world. Could it be the case, for example, that technologies from these two vast areas are more appropriate than those from the West, because they are generated in a more labour-abundant and capital-scarce environment (following the logic of the so-called induced innovation theory)? Or, are the assumptions of this theory not widely met in the Africa context? These questions are addressed with particular reference to the Chinese involvement in African manufacturing (see Chapter 8).

Then, finally, there is a policy chapter (5) on promoting labour-intensive techniques in African manufacturing. Many studies have shown that such techniques are more efficient at the prevailing factor prices in much of the region. Yet, paradoxically, these techniques tend, as noted earlier, to be overlooked in the selection process, which favours instead large-scale, capital-and import-intensive alternatives. Though others have investigated the reasons for this seemingly irrational behaviour, my focus is on the extent of institutional change (or institutional trait-making). Using concepts borrowed from Hirschman (1967), I try to identify exactly which traits need to be made and how this can be achieved. Such an exercise can be usefully thought of as the choice of technology in a 'three-factor world'. (See Chapter 9.)

What cannot be ignored in this regard is the potential role of small-scale enterprises in African manufacturing. For, not only do such firms dominate employment in this sector, but also they are also prone to making highly labour-intensive technical choices. Not all such firms, however, are efficient, and ways need to be found of growing the more dynamic of them into the formal sector (see Chapter 5). From there they will hopefully grow and increase the demand for labour in manufacturing. Much can be learnt in this regard from Chinese 'plug and play' export processing zones designed for small-scale firms.

The chapters to follow are divided into three related parts. The first deals with the problems of structural change in Africa from both a historical and contemporary perspective. The Lewis model is used as a framework to bring together both the supply and demand aspects of the problem, which are shown to be formidable and will probably lead in the future to ever higher rates of unemployment, poverty and inequality. These socio-economic phenomena in turn will tend only to exacerbate an already severe situation and could lead to further violent crime and instability in the area. The second part of the book is concerned with the countervailing tendencies that might skew the future outcome in a more favourable direction. I am referring here, for example, to the possibility of relatively labour-intensive industrial technologies from China and India and the role of services in a potentially new model of structural change. The two chapters in the final part continue with the technological theme of the previous chapters and deal in particular with the crucial and recently neglected topic of building technological capabilities in Africa. Chapter 11 is concerned with the main findings, directions for further research and conclusions for policy.

Notes

1   Many countries are of course also rich in resources.
2   It is interesting in this regard to trace *The Economist*'s changing view of African development prospects. After glowing talk of 'Africa rising' (2013) and an 'awakening giant' (2014), the magazine has most recently adopted a more sombre view (2015). One of its main concerns is that 'the African manufacturing sector's contribution to the continent's total economy actually declined from 12% to 11%' (2015:35) over the period from 1980 to 2013, 'leaving it with the smallest share of any developing region' (2015:35). This article concludes, 'There is a long road ahead for Africa to emulate East Asia' (2015:35).
3   *The Economist* cites McMillan to the effect that 'manufacturing has become less labour intensive across the board' (2015:35). If my analysis to follow is correct, this tendency will only become worse over time, subject, perhaps, to countervailing influence from China and India.

Part I

Defining the issues

2 Structural change in historical perspective

In the previous chapter I took note of the fact that for much of the past 15 years, total output in Africa has been growing at a rate of around 5 per cent per annum. (I also observed, however, that in per capita terms, this record is much less impressive.) From a dual-economy perspective, an assessment of the durability of Africa's growth depends in part on the pattern of sectoral change with which it has been associated. What matters, in particular, is whether the changes in sectoral shares of output have been growth-inducing or growth-retarding, i.e. whether resources have moved from low to high-productivity sectors or whether they have moved in the opposite direction (McMillan, Rodrik, & Verdusco-Gallo, 2014).

In this chapter I review the record of structural change in Africa over, say, the past 15 years, from the point of view of the dual-economy model as this was described above; that is, from the perspective of the changes in the GDP accounted for by manufacturing.[1] I am referring here not just to this sector in the aggregate, but also, and equally crucially, to its component parts.

The nature and scope of the problem

Part of the structural change envisaged by Lewis has occurred in Africa over the past decade or two. I am referring here to the decline in the share of agriculture as reported in Table 2.1.

The other part of the dual-economy model, however, has failed to materialise. In particular, as shown in Table 2.1, the share of manufacturing in Africa has fallen quite sharply, rather than increased as predicted. On the other hand, the services sector has grown and the formal part of it will have taken up part of the growth-inducing role that has not been played by manufacturing in the generally positive African growth experience of the past 20 years. The key question remains though, of whether there are sufficient productive and tradeable service activities to ensure that growth on the continent can retain or even increase its current level in the absence of a 'revolution' in manufacturing. I shall return to this question in a later chapter (Chapter 7).

It is also disturbing from the dual-economy perspective that the changes in sectoral shares noted above have not generally been accompanied by economic growth; on the contrary, movements of labour have been on balance from high to low-productivity operations rather than the other way round. For example, workers may have moved from relatively productive jobs in manufacturing to unproductive

Table 2.1 Change in sectoral shares (selected periods)

Sector	Period	% Change
Agriculture & services	1990–2010	'The main sectoral output movements that have occurred over this period involve a reduction in the agricultural output share by about 8 percentage points combined with a corresponding rise in the share of services' (Fox et al., 2013:5).
Agriculture & services	2005–2009	Over this period, the agricultural share of GDP fell from 16.9 to 12.7, while the services share rose from 51.7 to 56.6 (OECD, nd).
Manufacturing	1990–2008	Over this period, manufacturing's share of GDP fell from 15.3 to 10.5 (UNIDO, 2011:15).
Manufacturing	2005–2013	Share of manufacturing fell from 11.5 to 9 (African Development Bank, 2014).
Mining and utilities	1990–2008	The share of mining and utilities grew from 15.2 to 25.8 (UNIDO, 2011:15).

Sources: As reported in table.

informal employment in the services sector. This could easily have been the result of globalisation: workers from inefficient local firms in the former sector being forced as a result of global competition to take up low-paying jobs in the latter. Indeed, more generally 'globalization appears not to have fostered the desirable kind of structural change. Labor has moved in the direction, from more productive to less productive activities, including, most notably, informality' (McMillan, Rodrik & Verdusco-Gallo, 2014:2).[2]

For McMillan, Rodrik and Verdusco-Gallo (2014), the findings reported in the previous paragraph are not at all what they might have expected. For,

> if there is one region where we would have expected the flow of labor from traditional to modern parts of the economy to be an important driver of growth, a la dual-economy models, that surely is Africa. The disappointment is all the greater in light of all of the reforms that African countries have undergone since the late 1980s.
>
> (McMillan, Rodrik and Verdusco-Gallo, 2014:12)

Much depends according to these authors, on three determining factors, the first of which is whether the country has a 'revealed advantage in primary products'. The more that it does, the less likely is growth-inducing structural change to occur.

> The key here is that minerals and natural resources do not generate much employment, unlike manufacturing industries and related services. Even though these "enclave" sectors typically operate at very high productivity, they cannot absorb the surplus labour from agriculture.
>
> (McMillan, Rodrik and Verdusco-Gallo, 2014:3)

The second determining factor is whether countries resist the temptation to overvalue their currencies and keep them instead at competitive levels (thus effectively subsidising tradeable goods and services). Finally, and again intuitively, McMillan, Rodrik and Verdusco-Gallo (2014) find that labour-market flexibility makes for more growth-inducing structural change, since it is then easier for workers to move across sectors in the manner postulated by dual-economy models.

Regional groupings of countries

Lest it be thought that the decline in the share of manufacturing is confined to just parts of the African continent, Table 2.2 shows that, on the contrary, it happens uniformly across all the main regions. It is, in other words, a continent-wide problem when viewed from the perspective of the dual-economy approach.

From the table it appears that the biggest declines were registered in Middle (11.2 to 6.4 per cent) and in Western Africa (from 13 to 5.0 per cent), over the period 1990 to 2008. In terms of levels, the contribution of manufacturing to GDP had declined to below 10 per cent in three out of the four areas with the notable exception of Southern Africa (with a relatively large share of nearly 20 per cent). This exceptional performance is due in large part to the presence in that region of relatively industrialised countries such as South Africa, Botswana and Namibia.

Note, by way of contrast:

> The economic structure has changed more swiftly among LICs [low-income countries] in East Asia with the agricultural output ratio falling by 15 percentage points of GDP. Moreover, in contrast to the experience in SSA, the industrial sector has made a large contribution to the output transformation. The manufacturing output share has risen by 4 percentage points in low income East Asian countries, and in the lower middle income countries, the manufacturing share continued to increase ... More importantly, in East Asian low-middle income (LMI) countries, by 2010 manufactured output accounted for about twice the corresponding output of sub-Saharan Africa.
>
> (Fox et al., 2013:5)

Table 2.2 Regional changes in the share of manufacturing 1990–2008

Region	Contribution of manufacturing to GDP (%)			
	1990	2000	2005	2008
Eastern Africa	13.4	10.4	10.3	9.7
Middle Africa	11.2	8.2	7.3	6.4
Southern Africa	22.9	18.4	17.9	18.2
Western Africa	13.1	7.8	6.0	5.0

Source: UNIDO, 2011:15.

A comparison between African and Asian countries is also useful in calculating what Page (2012) refers to as Africa's 'structural deficit'. By this he means a measure of the degree of structural change that would be required for this region to earn the label of 'middle-income', according to the World Bank classification of countries. For this purpose, Page proposes a benchmark with reference to that institution's definition of lower-middle-income countries, namely, those with a GDP per capita of between $996 and $3,495 at 2009 prices. 'Thus, the benchmark economy was constructed by averaging the sectoral shares of value added and employment in a sample of countries at the time at which they crossed the USD 996 middle-income threshold' (Page, 2012:89).

On this basis, the author chooses the following seven Asian countries, with the dates of their transition to lower middle-income status in parentheses: China (2000), India (2007), Indonesia (2004), Korea (1968), Malaysia (1968), Philippines (1976) and Thailand (1987). Sectoral values, comprising an average of these seven countries, are then compared with a 'typical' low-income African economy. Tellingly, from a dual-economy perspective, Page notes that

> the most striking difference occurs in manufacturing where the value-added share and the labour share are about half of the benchmark value. It is also striking that the relative labour productivity of manufacturing is below that of the benchmark, suggesting that little productivity growth has taken place within the manufacturing sector in Africa compared to the benchmark countries.
>
> (Page, 2012:89)

There is, however, a positive aspect to this disappointing outcome. It is that the estimated shortfall for low-income Africa constitutes a major opportunity, in that structural change could yield a substantial growth dividend, as it already has in numerous Asian countries. In order to derive some idea of the magnitude of these gains, Page performs an interesting thought experiment. Specifically, assume with him, that productivity differences between sectors in the 'typical' African low-income country remain the same, but that employment between sectors changes in line with the benchmark level. The result would be that

> On average economy-wide productivity for the low-income African countries would increase 1.3 times. Ethiopia's productivity would increase 1.6 times, Malawi's 2.2 times, and Zambia's 1.8 times ... *These numbers are indicative of the extent of dualism that marks the region's economies.*
>
> (Page, 2012: 92; emphasis added)

Country variation

Obviously, there will be more variation at the country level. Table 2.3, for example, shows the ten best – and ten worst – performing African countries in terms of manufacturing growth in value-added over the period 1990 to 2010.

Note, first, that while the group of worst-performers is dominated by resource-rich countries, as one might expect, there are also four such countries among the

Table 2.3 Variation in manufacturing growth performance 1990–2010

Manufacturing value added per capita (compound annual growth rate) Top ten countries	%	Manufacturing value added per capita (compound annual growth rate) Bottom ten countries	%
Namibia	6.9★	Rwanda	-5.9
Mozambique	6.2	Dom. Rep. Congo	-5.7★
Uganda	5.6	Zimbabwe	-5.5★
Angola	4.8★	Liberia	-3.6
Lesotho	4.3	Mali	-3.3★
Seychelles	2.8	Burundi	-2.9
Sudan	2.8	Sierra Leone	-2.4★
Nigeria	2.4	Guinea-Bissau	-2.2
Tanzania	2.2★	Chad	-1.8★
Mauritius	2.2★	Central African Rep.	-1.3★

Source: UNIDO, 2011:28.
★= resource-rich (at least a quarter of export earnings derived from natural resources).

group of high-performers. Apparently, being relatively reliant on natural resources is not an insuperable constraint to rapid growth in manufacturing value-added per capita. Note also that the data shown in Table 2.3 form part of a broader (UNIDO) taxonomy of industrial growth in Africa between the years 1990 and 2010.

The typology contains levels and rates of change: the former are measured by manufacturing value added per capita and the latter by the compound annual growth rate of manufacturing value added (as set out for 20 countries in Table 2.3). Basing its calculations on these two dimensions, UNIDO (2011) identifies five country groupings. The first, described as 'forerunners', includes countries that have a level of manufacturing that is at least twice the African average and a rate of growth of manufacturing value-added per capita that is at least 2.5 per cent. The second group, consisting of 'achievers', has attained a comparatively high level of manufacturing development but their rates of growth are below the 2.5 per cent cut-off level. 'Catching-up' countries have a lower level of manufacturing than the 'achievers', but they enjoy a higher-growth rate of this sector than the latter. The fourth category contains countries that are 'falling behind', that is, they exhibit similar levels of manufacturing value added to those in the previous group, but show, at the same time, a lower growth rate. Finally, the countries at an 'infant stage' are the polar opposite of the 'forerunners', exhibiting both very low levels of manufacturing and very low growth rates of this sector.

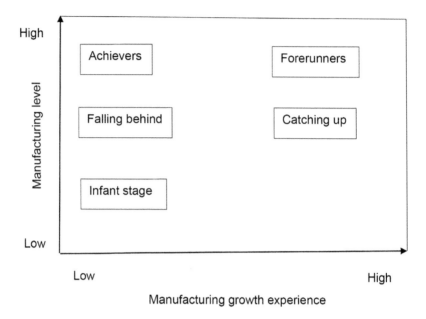

Figure 2.1 A typology of African countries.

Source: UNIDO, 2011:45.

Figure 2.1 shows these various possibilities diagrammatically, along the two dimensions noted above.

The variation in countries is most pronounced between 'forerunners' and those at an 'infant stage'. The former group in fact is represented by just two nations, the Seychelles and Namibia. The former country boasts the highest level of manufacturing among all the sample countries and an above-average growth of this sector, while the latter is a combination of the highest growth rate and an above-average level (see the appendix to this chapter for a full classification of the sample countries). The category comprising those at an 'infant stage', by contrast, contains a relatively large number of 'least developed' nations which exhibit both very poor levels and rates of growth of manufacturing. This category, incidentally, contains all but one of the countries listed in the right-hand column of Table 2.3. From among the many cases of unsuccessful manufacturing that are described as being in an 'infant stage', however, there are some notable bright spots. Chief among them, arguably, is Africa's fastest-growing economy, Ethiopia, which has recently attracted foreign investment in footwear and other manufactures, partly on the basis of a pro-gramme of industrial parks (World Bank, 2015c; *The Economist*, 2015a).[3]

The factor-intensity of manufacturing

The previous section dealt with the performance of the manufacturing sector as a whole. There was no attempt there to disaggregate the sector into its component parts. But from the dual-economy perspective, the factor-intensity of manufacturing

– especially its labour-intensity – is also key because one of the ultimate goals of the expansion of the modern sector is to create a large amount of productive employment. And in this wider context as well, there is much cause for concern.

Consider, to begin with, that the most labour-intensive sectors in manufacturing are the following (in descending order of labour-intensity):

- Apparel
- Textiles
- Wood
- Fabricated metals
- Food and beverages

(UNIDO, 2013)

These are the sectors in which much of Africa, with its relative abundance of unskilled and low-cost labour, would be expected to possess a comparative advantage (this is especially likely to be the case, one should note, in the region's least developed countries). Yet, on the whole, these and other light manufactures have not performed at all well. According to a World Bank Report in 2012, for example,

> While China's emergence in the global manufacturing market since 1980 has resulted in a broad decline in the market share of all regions, the decline in Sub-Saharan Africa's share has been longer and deeper than most. Sub-Saharan Africa's share of global light manufacturing has continually declined – to less than 1 percent – and preferential access to U.S. and European Union (EU) markets has made little difference'[4].

(Dinh et al., 2012:1)

Indeed, the report concludes that 'without structural transformation, Sub-Saharan Africa is unlikely to catch up with more prosperous countries like China and Vietnam, which were not very different from Sub-Saharan Africa in the 1980s' (Dinh et al., 2012:1–2).

The comparison with Asia becomes clearer in Table 2.4, which indicates the share of light manufactures in total exports for selected Asian and African countries 1990–1994 and 2005–2010. Some of the former countries exhibited a fall in the share of these goods over the period, partly, one suspects, as the result of a move towards more capital-intensive products. Others, however, such as Cambodia and Vietnam, experienced a sharp rise in the percentage share of light manufactures. What is notable about the three African economies shown in the table has partly to do with the lack of change between the two periods, and also and relatedly with the low level compared with the Asian countries even at the end of the period. Consider, in this regard, a comparison between Zambia and Cambodia. In the former, the share of light manufactures in total exports is only 3 per cent compared to the figure for Cambodia of 89 per cent.

There are, of course, exceptions to this general pattern, with the case of Mauritius being probably the most notable. This country established a garment and textile industry in 1968 following Independence (Frankel, 2010) and it formed the core of

Table 2.4 Share of light manufactures in total exports in selected Asian and African
          countries, 1990–1994 and 2005–2009

Country	% *1990–1994*	% *2005–2009*
Bangladesh	81	91
China	56	35
Ethiopia	10	9
Indonesia	19	16
India	41	29
Cambodia	21	89
Lao	32	22
Pakistan	73	71
Tanzania	10	6
Vietnam	21	43
Zambia	2	3

the trade-led growth in the 1970s and beyond. Indeed, by the end of the 1990s the
country had already been carried into what Frankel refers to as 'tiger status'. Quite
what has enabled this to occur is a matter of ongoing debate, but it may well have had
to do in part with the role of export-processing zones (EPZs), which in turn owed
their successful operations to 'good institutions' (Frankel, 2010). Certainly, Mauritius
ranks highly on some of the well-known measures of institutional performance such
as political participation, the rule of law and containment of corruption.

Frankel's conclusions from that country's experiences, are, predictably, of an
institutional character. One is that 'a well-designed electoral system can accom-
modate ethnic diversity – even harness it productively', while the other is that
'democracies can achieve economic reform, and perhaps in a more sustainable way
than autocracies' (Frankel, 2010:28). The third lesson for other African countries –
a familiar economics argument – is that trade is the key determinant of growth,
especially in small countries. Unfortunately, this last lesson is not one that has been
well absorbed by African governments, especially in relation to light manufactures.
Indeed, according to Dinh et al. (2012:32)

> no-one – not policy makers, academics, or donors – paid enough attention to
> light manufacturing. African nations made little effort to smooth the path for
> would-be private entrepreneurs, neglecting lessons from the post-World War II
> experience of numerous formerly low-income economies … that have leveraged
> the achievements of private sector manufacturers to promote national prosperity.
>   (Dinh et al., 2012:32)

This, one should emphasise, is part of a broader pattern of neglect involving technology and technological capabilities. Investments in public sector projects, for example, have generally been conceived ab initio as large-scale and capital-intensive (see section below), without regard to their implications for inequality and poverty, or their effects on technological capabilities and learning. Public enterprises were largely dismantled during the structural adjustment period in Africa, but this did not automatically mean that any greater attention was paid to technology by privately owned firms. For, the technological system in which they are embedded continues to lack an effective technological component of the kind established in a number of Asian countries (see, for example, Lall, 1996): that is, one that establishes various effective links among, for example, producers, research institutes and government technology institutes. Overall, and even now, I can only agree with Pietrobelli when he argues that 'the biggest policy gap in Africa is perhaps the lack of official appreciation of how important technological development is to manufacturing growth and competitiveness' (Pietrobelli, 2006).

The choice of technology in manufactures

It is not enough to discuss only the factor intensity of different branches of manufacturing. For, within a given branch, there is often a wide variety of available production techniques, which can vary quite considerably in terms of their factor-intensity. The choice of such techniques has important implications for employment creation, as I will seek to show in the following chapter. The point there will be that in spite of the availability of efficient labour-intensive alternatives, there is a puzzling tendency for producers to opt instead for much more import – and capital – intensive processes.

The choice of technology can be simply depicted in the graphical form of Figure 2.2.

Each point on the curve (an isoquant) represents the same level of output. Which point is chosen depends on the price ratio between capital and labour. In developed countries, where capital is relatively cheap, the isocost line is shown to be tangential to the isoquant at point A, where the capital-labour ratio is equal to K_1L_1. In developing countries, by contrast, where labour is cheap relative to capital, the point of tangency occurs at B with a capital-labour ratio of K_2L_2. The technology chosen in the latter countries creates an additional amount of employment equal to L_1L_2.

In the weaving industry, for example, the technology at A may represent a fully automatic, high-speed loom, whereas B depicts an older, semi-automatic alternative. The capital-labour ratio between the two alternatives – and hence the differential opportunity for employment generation – is striking. Indeed, the ratio for the former technology exceeds that for the latter by a factor of 22 (Pack, 1982). Moreover, in the developing country context, the more labour-intensive technology is often more profitable than the alternative.[5] Thus, to the seemingly pronounced extent to which the capital-intensive technology is used in Africa, there is a corresponding scope for increasing both efficiency and employment (but see Chapter 9 for what this would actually require in a more realistic world of 'three-factors').

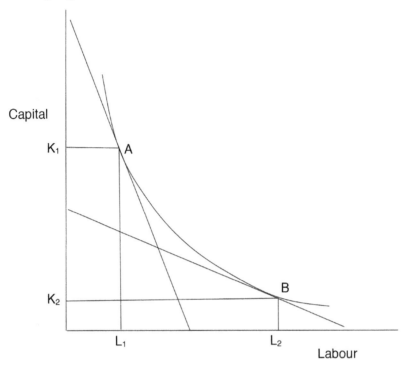

Figure 2.2 The choice of technology.
Source: UNIDO, 2011:45.

Note, finally, that differences in the factor intensity of manufacturing branches and technology choices within those branches may help to explain why there is quite a marked variation between the elasticity of employment with respect to output between certain African countries. Consider, for example, the elasticities shown in Table 2.5 for four such countries.[6]

Several patterns can be discerned in the data. One of them is that in general the employment elasticities have tended to decline over time. If this tendency holds across the continent as a whole, it is especially disquieting because of the rapid growth there of the labour force (see more on this below in Chapter 4) in almost all African countries.

A second observation is that 'Ethiopia and Ghana have been better able to translate GDP growth into employment increases, especially in the 2000s' (Martins, 2013:14). Though it is not supported by any evidence I am aware of, the hypothesis would be that these countries chose more labour-intensive branches of manufacturing and more labour-intensive technologies within those branches than did Mozambique and Tanzania. Alternatively, of course, it could be differences between, rather than within, sectors that underlie the findings shown in the table (agriculture, for example, is much less capital-intensive than mining). In actual fact, though, the real challenge may lie in a combination of things: increasing the

Table 2.5 Elasticities of employment with respect to output, selected African countries and periods

Country	1992–1996	1996–2000	2000–2004	2004–2008
Ethiopia	0.41	0.95	0.97	0.34
Ghana	0.64	0.64	0.52	0.40
Mozambique	0.56	0.29	0.29	0.32
Tanzania	1.04	0.64	0.23	0.27

share of manufacturing in total output, favouring labour-intensive branches within manufacturing and selecting more employment-intensive alternatives within each branch.

Employment and underemployment

Africa's failure to respond adequately to these various challenges stands in sharp contrast to the successful experience in certain Asian countries such as China and South Korea. It is reflected in a constant or declining share of manufactures in total output, the selection of relatively capital-intensive branches of manufacturing and labour-saving technologies within those branches. When it is combined with a fast-growing population (Fox et al., 2013), such limited demand for labour has meant far too few wage-paying jobs to absorb the new job seekers and those who are already underemployed in the informal part of the economy.

Table 2.6 for example, shows the extent of informality in selected African countries, even following a decade of relatively rapid output growth after 1995.

Note that the informal sector is defined in this table as agricultural labour, non-wage employment, and part-time wage employment (Golub & Hayat, 2014). Thus defined, it comprises at least 80 per cent in all countries and in about half the cases, over 90 per cent of total sectoral employment.[7] What concerns me about these figures is of course partly the widespread underemployment that so typifies work in the informal sector and the waste of resources that it implies. But I am also worried that there are in addition associated socio-political forces which may prevent even current growth rates in Africa from being realised in the future – see Chapter 4 for a full discussion of this argument. Of the utmost importance in that chapter will be the projected rates of growth in the youth population across the continent.

On the demand for labour side, a growing problem lies in the nature of technical progress over time. In particular, most new technology is developed in the rich countries, where labour is relatively scarce and receives a correspondingly high wage. Technical advances thus tend to be labour-saving in character and unsuitable for poor countries with a very different factor endowment and corresponding set of relative factor prices (Stewart, 1977). I am referring here, most obviously, but not exclusively, to innovations in information technology such as computer-aided design (CAD), computer aided manufacturing (CAM) and digital garment-printing

Table 2.6 Sectoral distribution of employment, selected African countries and years

Country (low-income Africa)	Year of survey	Public sector including state-owned enterprises (%)	Formal private sector (%)	Informal Sector (%)	Total (%)
Ghana	2010	6.4	7.0	86.6	100
Mali	2007	3.1	0.4	96.5	100
Rwanda	2006	3.7	1.2	95.1	100
Tanzania	2006	3.0	1.5	95.5	100
Uganda	2006	2.8	14.2	83.0	100
Ethiopia	2005	3.9	6.2	89.9	100
Cameroon	2005	4.9	4.7	90.4	100
Zambia	2005	5.2	6.8	88.0	100
Nigeria	2004	8.0	0.3	91.8	100

Source: Golub & Hayat, 2014:14.

machines. These and other labour-saving innovations may reduce the demand for unskilled labour even in the most employment-intensive industries such as textiles and garments. Of course, poor African countries do not *have* to choose inappropriate technologies, but they are often pushed in this direction by Western consultants, machinery suppliers and aid donors (James, 1995). There is some hope that China's heavy involvement in manufacturing on the continent will ameliorate this problem, because it has a different set of factor prices compared to developed countries and may thus generate more appropriate technological alternatives (see Chapter 6 for a discussion of this possibility). However, the empirical evidence on the issue is scant, as indeed is the current writing on technological choices in African industry.

Inequality and poverty

The pattern of employment and underemployment that has just been described is closely related to the extent of inequality and poverty on the African continent. That picture is one in which a relatively small number of highly paid jobs in the formal sector coexist with a vast amount of low-paying work in the much larger informal sector. There is, that is to say, a sizeable gap in the earnings of those who are located in these two sectors. Thus, 'Public enterprise and to a lesser extent general government earnings are particularly high, well above formal private sector earnings, which in turn are typically double to triple informal sector earnings, except in Madagascar, where the differential is lower' (Golub & Hayat, 2014:4).

The predictable result of findings such as these is a relatively high degree of inequality in the distribution of income, and this indeed is broadly what one finds. For

Africa as a whole, that is, the Gini ratio increased from 0.52 in 1993 to 0.56 in 2008 (Beegle et al., 2016). This average figure is high by developing-country standards, and especially by those that have adopted a more labour-intensive development strategy. The African average, moreover, conceals some pronounced regional variations. For example, inequality is most pronounced in Southern Africa (notably, in Botswana, Lesotho, Namibia, South Africa, Swaziland and Zambia, where Gini ratios are well above 0.6) (Beegle et al., 2016).

Inequality, in its turn, leads to a lower degree of poverty reduction for any given growth rate.

> Africa's high inequality substantially reduces the poverty-reducing effects of its growth.... The strong erosive effect of high initial inequality on the poverty-reducing powers of growth highlights the need for more inclusive growth processes and where possible even redistribution through safety nets and transfers, to accelerate Africa's poverty reduction in the future.
>
> (World Bank, 2013b-2.6)[8]

Deindustrialisation

In the sense of a declining share of manufacturing in output, I have already referred to deindustrialisation (see Table 2.2). At the international level, this phenomenon manifests itself as a falling share of manufactures in total exports. The tendency towards deindustrialisation internationally is illustrated with reference to Table 2.7, for a few selected African countries and in a small group of Asian comparators.

Table 2.7 Manufactured exports as a percentage of total exports, selected Asian and African countries 1990–1994 and 2005–2009

Country	*Manufactured exports as % total exports, 1990–1994 and 2005–2009*	
	1990–94	2005–09
Bangladesh	84	93
China	81	90
Indonesia	27	38
Cambodia	22	90
Vietnam	23	58
Ethiopia	22	13
Tanzania	13	12
Zambia	3	6

Source: Dinh et al., 2012:34.

I emphasise that these data are illustrative rather than representative of the regions from which they are drawn. Still, the differences are striking: all the Asian countries experienced quite rapid increases, in some cases of a spectacular kind, in the percentage share of manufactures, whereas two of the African nations experienced a fall. The third, Zambia, saw a modest increase from a minute base. By the end of the period, the differences in the shares of manufacturing between the countries in the two regions were acute (compare, say, Bangladesh with Zambia).

Yet another sense in which one may speak of deindustrialisation is closely derived from the dual-economy model. It occurs when industrial employment grows less than 1 per cent more rapidly than the labour force (Lewis, 1979). For then the surplus labour in the traditional sector will continue to grow. Lewis cautions that 'the surest way to run into trouble is to have "de-industrialisation" (industrial employment growing more slowly than the labour force), since this means that the reservoir of cheap labour will be filling instead of emptying' (Lewis, 1979:220). He further recognises, presciently, that this may have political and social as well as economic implications for society, since these factors depend on a 'continual flow' of labour from the 'reservoir' to the more productive sectors, rather than a 'relative expansion' of the informal sector.

Unlike the forms of deindustrialisation discussed thus far, 'premature de-industrialisation' as described by Rodrik (2015) is *defined* with reference to other countries. It is premature in the sense that industrialisation peaks at an income level well below what is found when the same event occurred among now developed countries. For example, 'Industrialization peaked in Western European countries such as Britain, Sweden and Italy at income levels of around $14,000 (in 1990 dollars). India and many sub-Saharan African countries appear to have reached their peak manufacturing employment shares at income levels of $700' (Rodrik, 2015:15). Put another way, the problem is that 'since 1990 countries have reached peak manufacturing employment at incomes that are around a third of the levels experienced before 1990. For MVA [manufacturing value added] at constant prices, the corresponding ratio is *less* than a half' (Rodrik, 2015:16, emphasis in original).

Prematurely aborted industrialisation, according to the author,

> is not good news for developing nations. It blocks off the main avenue of rapid convergence in low-income settings, the shift of workers from the countryside to urban factories where their productivity tends to be much higher. Industrialization contributes to growth both because of this reallocation effect and because manufacturing tends to experience relatively stronger productivity growth over the medium to longer term. In fact, organized, formal manufacturing appears to exhibit unconditional convergence, ... which makes it special and an engine of growth.
>
> (Rodrik, 2015:23)

One solution to the problem, as Rodrik sees it, is to rely instead on relatively productive and tradeable services, but whether this is likely to represent a viable alternative is a question I postpone until Chapter 7.

Conclusions

From a dual-economy perspective, African growth since 1995 has left much to be desired, despite the relatively high increases in output (by past standards) that have been achieved on average. Most notably, formal sector manufacturing has fallen as a percentage of GDP, as have manufactured exports as a percentage of total exports.[9] The problem is especially pronounced in light manufacturing, an area where Africa might, most especially, be expected to possess a comparative advantage. These typically labour-intensive products (such as textiles and garments) have, however, tended to fall as a share of total value added and as a percentage of total exports. Within particular branches of manufacturing, moreover, labour-intensive (appropriate) techniques have rarely been selected over large-scale, import – and capital – intensive alternatives. Altogether, it appears as if manufacturing – and especially light-manufactures – has been largely ignored as a means of achieving structural change, in the ways that have characterised the successful development of numerous newly developed and certain Asian countries. Instead, the result has been widespread deindustrialisation and premature deindustrialisation, leading to pervasive underemployment and persistent (indeed, increased absolute numbers of those living in) poverty.

In the next chapter, I investigate which specific assumptions of the Lewis dual-economy model have been violated in Africa, and describe how these assumptions need to be amended. It is the amended model, I maintain, that is relevant to understanding contemporary African industrialisation and discerning what needs to be done about it.

Appendix

Table 2A.1 Classification of countries according to industrialisation level and growth rate

Country	Classification
Seychelles	Forerunners
Namibia	Forerunners
Mauritius	Achievers
South Africa	Achievers
Swaziland	Achievers
Gabon	Achievers
Lesotho	Catching up
Angola	Catching up
Mozambique	Catching up
Sudan	Catching up
Uganda	Catching up
Botswana	Falling behind

(continued)

Table 2A.1 Continued

Country	Classification
Cameroon	Falling behind
Cote d'Ivoire	Falling behind
Congo	Falling behind
Senegal	Falling behind
Kenya	Falling behind
Zambia	Falling behind
Burkina Faso	Falling behind
Tanzania	Falling behind
Ghana	Falling behind
Zimbabwe	Falling behind
Madagascar	Falling behind
Nigeria	Falling behind
Benin	Falling behind
Mauritania	Falling behind
Rwanda	Infant stage
Guinea–Bissau	Infant stage
Chad	Infant stage
CAR	Infant stage
Malawi	Infant stage
Guinea	Infant stage
Niger	Infant stage
Burundi	Infant stage
Ethiopia	Infant stage
Eritrea	Infant stage
Somalia	Infant stage
Mali	Infant stage
Sierra Leone	Infant stage
DRC	Infant stage
Liberia	Infant stage

Source: UNIDO, 2011:46.

Notes

1 Though it may once have been understandable to confine one's attention to this sector, it is nowadays too confining, as Page (2012) has pointed out. In particular,

> Changes in the global economy ... make the tendency to associate industry with manufacturing potentially misleading in both analytical and policy terms. Falling transport and communications costs have created a class of economic activities in agriculture and services that more closely resemble manufacturing than the sectors to which they are assigned in economic statistics.... The global agricultural value chain in flowers and horticultural crops provides an example. (Page, 2012:94)

2 An estimate of the size of the informal sector in Africa, is contained in Golub & Hayat (2014).

3 The experience of Mauritius with textiles and apparel is also worth noting (Frankel, 2010). Indeed, this country is, after South Africa, the next most industrialised in Africa (UNIDO, 2013). Consider too, Ethiopia's successful venture in selling cut flowers in the markets of the European Union (Dinh et al., 2012).

It is worth noting too the ILO's observation that

> 'the quality of jobs is of considerable concern, with working poverty and vulnerable employment the highest across all regions. In particular, nearly eight out of ten employed persons in Sub-Saharan Africa were in vulnerable forms of employment. Accordingly, the vulnerable employment rate – the share of own-account workers and unpaid family workers in total employment – was estimated at 76.6 per cent in 2014, significantly higher than the global average of 45.3 per cent'
>
> (ILO, 2015:53).

According to another ILO report (2014) the vulnerable employment rate in Africa as a whole decreased by only 2.3 percentage points between 2001 and 2012.

4 It is worth emphasising here that even the share of the two most labour-intensive branches of manufacturing – textiles and apparel – saw a decline over the period 2000 to 2009 in total African manufacturing value-added (UNIDO, 2011:10).

5 During the period when African manufacturing was dominated by state-owned enterprises, the bias towards capital-intensity was especially marked, although it was also noticeable in relation to privately owned firms (James, 1995).

6 Bear in mind here the equation that $\dfrac{K}{L} = \dfrac{K}{O}\dfrac{O}{L}$.

7 It is important not to take too monolithic a view of the informal sector. While there are indeed many cases of underemployment and low productivity, there are also a number of dynamic small firms that are on their way into the formal sector (see Chapter 5).

8 According to Chandy (2015), the number of people in Africa living on less than $1.25 per day increased from 358 million in 1996 to 415 million in 2011. The share of poverty in the total population, however, has *fallen*.

9 Note that much of African growth has been heavily driven by a rise in the price of exports of natural resources since 2000. Indeed, exports of this kind make up nearly three-quarters of this regional total. The problem is that resource-rich countries typically do not engage in structural transformation involving an increase in the share of manufacturing. See World Bank (2013b).

3 The Lewis model in alternative historical contexts

In the first chapter I defended the basic dual-economy framework as a means of understanding structural transformation in Africa. Thereafter, in Chapter 2, this framework was used to analyse the progress of manufacturing in that region since about 1995. The current chapter draws on those before it, but it also differs from them in two major respects. One is that it is explicitly comparative, containing a direct comparison between the Lewis model in the history of the now industrialised countries and certain East Asian economies on the one hand, and the recent African experience on the other. The second difference is methodological: this chapter relies on a series of simple diagrams to illustrate the main issues under consideration (which are mostly about the supply to, and the demand for, labour by the formal sector of the economy). Subsequently, in the next chapter, I try to make the graphical analysis more concrete by providing some approximate estimates of the future supply and demand for labour in African manufacturing. The conclusions drawn there give rise to serious concerns about the social and political sustainability of the current approach to that sector. The chapters in the second part of the book, however, suggest that these concerns may be ameliorated by a set of countervailing forces on the demand side of the labour market.

The Lewis model

The widely cited model first published by Lewis in 1954, turns on the notion of an unlimited (or perfectly elastic) supply of labour to the modern (or capitalistic) sector of the economy. This condition obtains, according to Lewis when,

> Population is so large relatively to capital and natural resources, that there are large sectors of the economy where the marginal productivity of labour is negligible, zero, or even negative. Several writers have drawn attention to the existence of such 'disguised unemployment' in the agricultural sector, demonstrating in each case that the family holding is so small that if some members of the family obtained other employment the remaining members could cultivate the holding just as well.

(Lewis, 1954:141)

The agriculture sector thus forms part of the 'informal' sector which operates mainly on non-capitalist lines (such as when there is family ownership). Lewis is at pains to point out, however, that the informal sector contains more economic activity than goes on only in farming. Also included, for example, is the whole range of casual labour (such as 'petty retail trading') that is typically so visible in developing countries.

Growth in the model occurs as the formal sector absorbs surplus labour (with lower productivity) from the rest of the economy, as shown in Figure 3.1.

The process begins with OL units of labour employed in the formal sector at a wage equal to Ow. The supply of labour is perfectly elastic at this wage because of the labour surplus in the non-formal sector of the economy. The initial demand for labour curve (which represents the marginal product of this factor) is given by AA and intersects the supply curve at P, the initial equilibrium.

Profits, given by the area APw, are then reinvested,[1] and the AA curve shifts uniformly outward to BB (I shall deal shortly with the implications of a non-uniform shift in the AA curve). The new profits are reinvested and the process continues until point J is reached on the supply curve, which denotes that surplus labour is exhausted and wages need to be increased in order to attract additional workers (the so-called Lewis turning point). Apart from the initial size of the formal sector, whose role was discussed in an earlier chapter, the speed at which the process

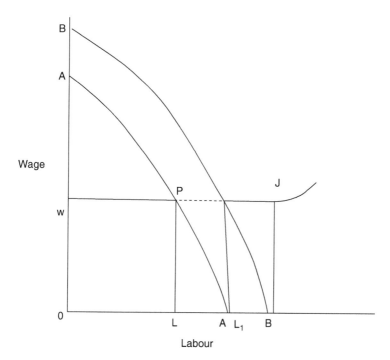

Figure 3.1 Growth in the basic Lewis model.

Source: Based on Lewis, 1954.

operates depends on both the shape of the new demand curve for labour and the extent of labour-force growth, which determines the pace at which the 'turning point' occurs (i.e., when the labour supply curve turns upwards).

Shape of the new demand curve

Consider in Figure 3.2 the different ways in which the capital to labour ratio may behave as output expands (along the so-called expansion path)

Three types of technical change are identified in the figure. The first, impliclty assumed by Lewis in 1954, is that the capital–labour ratio stays constant as output increases (so-called neutral technical progress). In the other two cases, the ratio either increases ('labour-saving' technological progress) or decreases ('capital-saving' technological progress).

Corresponding to each form of technical change is a particular shape of the demand for labour curve. BB from Figure 3.1, for example, indicates the neutral form, and this curve also reappears in Figure 3.3, along with the two other possibilities from Figure 3.2.

As before, BB represents the uniform outward shift of the AA curve, resulting from neutral technological change. Now, in addition, two extra curves are shown, BB_1 and BB_2, representing, respectively, labour-saving and capital-saving technical change. Note that in the extreme case BB_1 will intersect the labour-supply

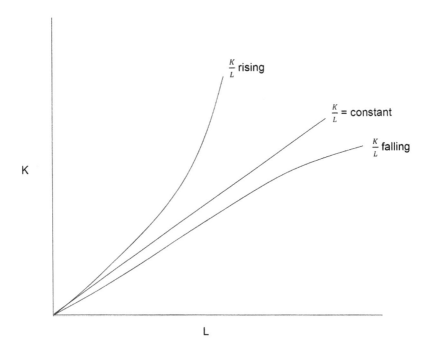

Figure 3.2 Expansion path: varying K/L ratio.

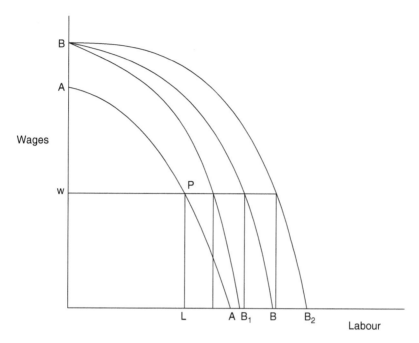

Figure 3.3 Forms of technical change and employment.

Source: Based on Lewis, 1954.

curve at P, and there will be *no* increase at all in jobs as output increases (so-called jobless growth). As expected, most extra jobs in the formal sector are associated with the curve representing capital-saving technical change, given by BB_2.

These, then, are the alternatives on the demand for labour side. I turn next to examine the possibilities with labour supply in the Lewis model.

Labour supply side

Assume for the sake of argument that the original demand for labour curve is given by BB, as before. What needs to be known about the supply line is where the turning-point occurs, since it is this that determines how many workers remain in the informal sector of the economy.

AA and BB are reproduced from Figure 3.1, and in the case where the supply curve turns upward at J, the entire labour force in the informal sector is absorbed (equal to OP). Where there is an increase in the labour force in the informal sector (due, say, to population growth), however, the turning point is assumed to occur only at K, and there remains surplus labour equal to PQ. That is, there has been an elongation of the supply of labour[2] compared to the initial position.

Combining the demand- and supply-side discussions leads to two limiting cases: one that conforms to the Lewis model and the other that departs most strikingly

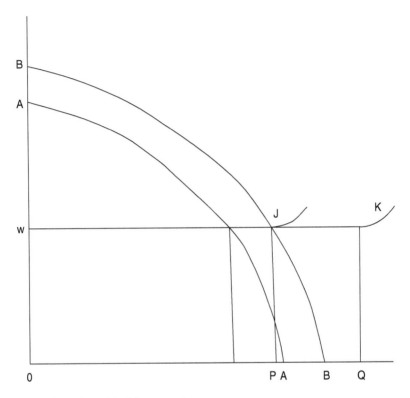

Figure 3.4 Elongation of the labour-supply curve.

Source: Based on Lewis, 1954.

from it. When I say conforms or disconfirms the model, I am referring to the conditions under which structural change is most or least likely to occur; that is, whether the surplus labour in the informal sector is more or less likely to be absorbed. Thus, for example, while there has to be enough of a labour surplus to cause a perfectly elastic labour supply curve, too many labourers beyond this point make it difficult for the absorption process to occur.

It is well to note here that most developing countries do not fall into either of the two limiting cases I have just described. For, although they still suffer to a greater or lesser extent from the demand-side problem of a rising capital–labour ratio in manufacturing (but see Chapter 6), the supply-side issue of rapid population growth is much less in evidence. In Table 3.2 below, for example, the population growth in Asia and Latin America is projected to be much less over the next 35 years than in Africa, where an average annual rate of over 2.5 per cent is expected. Other things being equal, therefore, it is likely to be in this last-mentioned continent that un- and underemployment, poverty and inequality will be most acutely felt in the coming decades. The following chapter assesses the extent to which these tendencies are likely to cause instability and conflict in the region.

Two limiting cases

Favourable supply and demand conditions

This case occurs when there is capital-saving (or neutral) technological progress combined with relatively few labourers in the non-formal sector of the economy, as shown in Figure 3.5. It will not take long in such an economy to reach the turning point at J.

The point here is that the rightward shift of the labour demand curve absorbs a relatively large number of those residing in the informal part of the economy, while in the next case the opposite occurs. It is worth stressing here again that an abundance of labour, as expressed by an elongated supply curve of labour, 'is not a condition to be desired' (Lewis, 1979:220). For, as Lewis (1979:220) put it, 'the political and social health of the community, no less than its economic health, requires a continual transfer from the reservoir to the more productive sector, rather than the relative expansion of the sector.'

The least favourable outcome

In this situation a labour-saving shift in the demand curve absorbs only a small fraction of the population outside the formal sector. Thus, there remains much to be done if the process of structural change is to work effectively. In particular, an amount of PQ units of labour needs still to be absorbed by the formal sector.

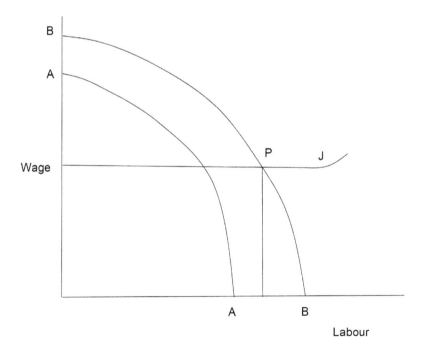

Figure 3.5 Favourable supply and demand conditions.
Source: Based on Lewis, 1954.

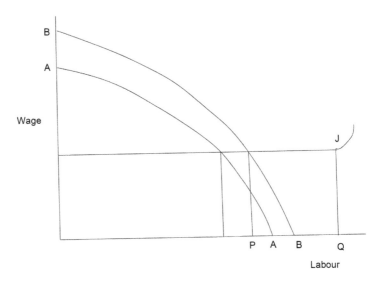

Figure 3.6 The least favourable outcome.
Source: Based on Lewis, 1954.

As regards the one limiting case, it is difficult to find in the economic history of the now developed countries or the still-remaining developing nations, instances where technical change was neutral or capital-saving and population growth was very low.[3] It is easier, as argued below, to find instances of this type of technical change in the history of the now developed countries and more recently by certain economies of East Asia. On the other hand, in the second limiting case discussed above, the African experience of the last 20 years is replete with examples of unusually high rates of population growth combined with heavily labour-saving technical progress, imported mostly from the developed countries.

The history of the now developed countries and East Asia

The pattern of technical change during the Industrial Revolution in Great Britain and the early-follower countries (such as the US and Germany) appears to have been somewhat responsive to the then prevailing condition of relative labour abundance. Evidence (admittedly sketchy) indicates, for example, that capital and labour grew at equivalent rates of 2.5 per cent in manufacturing during the early phase of the Industrial Revolution (von Tunzelmann, 1981). Technical change, that is to say, was broadly neutral over the period.

In the European early-follower countries, as well, deliberate efforts were made to exert a restraining influence on the growth of capital per head, as Landes (1965) has forcefully argued in the following terms:

> In Europe the follower countries made the most of their cheap manpower by building more rudimentary but less expensive equipment, buying second-hand

machines whenever possible, and concentrating on the more labor-intensive branches or stages of manufacture. Not until the last third of the century did the Continental economies conform to the usual theoretical model and avail themselves of the opportunity to adopt the latest techniques; and even then they maintained a larger working force per unit of production ... than Britain or the United States. In addition, they tended to be prodigal in their use of labor to manipulate or move materials and goods ... Finally, the Continental mills, like the early British factories, worked their equipment as long and hard as possible.

(Landes, 1965:116)

In a manner similar to what has just been described, technical progress in a number of successful East Asian countries, such as Korea, Taiwan and Japan, also took a discernibly labour-using form. In the first-mentioned country, for example, after the mid-1960s, 'Examples of capital-stretching adaptations of imported technology abound in textiles, electronics, and plywood production' (Ranis, 1973:402). Indeed, so intensive was the adaptation of imported technology in these and other industries, that for a part of the period after 1964, the capital-labour ratio in manufacturing was actually reduced in Korea (Ranis, 1973). In Japan, as well, this ratio remained essentially constant during the last part of the nineteenth century, indicating 'the effectiveness of capital-stretching innovations at the aggregate level' (Ranis, 1973:402).

Such favourable patterns of technical change as these, reflect, at least in part, a close conformity to the conditions for induced innovation (as these are discussed in Chapter 8). Perhaps chief among these were factor prices which accurately reflected factor scarcities, namely, a relative abundance of labour and a shortage of capital. Such prices, however, were made decisive in technological choices only because of the strategy of export promotion in manufactures, which drove firms to adopt cost-minimising behaviour. In Taiwan, for example,

with expensive capital, non-inflated urban wage rates, and a progressively more open economy from 1959 onward, large-scale firms began to turn to the manufacture of labor-intensive exports ... [and] every commercially feasible possibility for substituting labor for capital was exploited.

(Johnston & Kilby, 1975:315)

How, one might then ask, were East Asian exporters of manufactures to developed countries able to escape from the dictates of product quality, which are often associated with capital-intensive methods of production? Textiles and garments, for example, often depend for their quality on the precision of mechanised forms of technology (which have a low tolerance for errors of various kinds).[4] The answer, it seems to me, turns on the recognition that in developed, as indeed in other, countries there are in fact many different markets, differentiated among other ways, by incomes and preferences (Stewart, 1977).

Faced with a trade-off between price and quality, those with relatively low incomes may be more price conscious than those who are more affluent. In many of the major export markets, the East Asian countries appear to have competed at the lower ends – among those who are price rather than brand conscious. They competed, that is to say, largely among those who were 'too poor to be concerned with brand names' (Chenery & Keesing, 1979:25).

Concerns about the demands of product quality were also ameliorated by exporting to the less exacting markets of other developing countries. Amsden, for example, has noted how the sale of a lower-quality hand tool to Hong Kong and Southeast Asia 'suited the factor endowments prevailing in Taiwan at the time' (Amsden, 1977:219). A similar case has been reported for Hong Kong, where simpler, cheaper machinery was competing in 'what, in effect was a different, lower-income market' (Fransman, 1984:311).

In terms of their domestic economies as well, the group of East Asian follower countries was generally able to avoid the influence of an unequal income distribution on the demand for expensive, high-quality products. For, then, a small group of relatively affluent consumers is able to exert a powerful influence over the type of products that are produced, at the expense of the majority. But in fact during their periods of unprecedented growth, countries such as Taiwan, Korea and Japan enjoyed a relatively equal distribution (in contrast to Africa, where, generally, incomes are much more unequally distributed).

Africa as a limiting case

Africa has generally been found wanting in the favourable conditions that were so prevalent in East Asia, during the period of rapid industrialisation in countries such as Japan, Korea and Taiwan[5]. On both sides of the labour market, that is to say, conditions were, and mostly remain, inimical to the process of structural change.

On the demand side, for example, few and far between have been the efforts to modify capital-intensive technology imported from the developed countries. There are several reasons for this. One of them is that factor prices in Africa rarely reflect relative scarcities of capital and labour. This is, they are often markedly distorted. A typical problem is that wages are set at artificially high levels, reflecting, among other things, minimum wage legislation. As a result, as Clarke has pertinently observed:

> Unit labor costs are ... significantly higher than in successful manufacturing intensive economies of East Asia (China, Indonesia, Malaysia, Philippines, Thailand and Vietnam). The point estimate suggests that on average unit labor costs are about 20 percent lower on average in these countries than in Sub-Saharan Africa. This suggests that it will be more difficult for firms in Sub-Saharan Africa to compete with firms from these regions.
>
> (Clarke, 2012:9)

Artificially high wages,[6] moreover, have often been accompanied by an overly cheap cost of capital. During the 1970s and 1980s in South Africa, for example, there was a combination of rising wages and negative real interest rates, which, together with tax breaks for capital investment, encouraged firms across the whole economy to use more labour-saving techniques (Nattrass, 2003).

Even without factor price biases of this kind, moreover, it is doubtful that there were sufficient technological capabilities to effect the type of adaptations to technology that were listed above in relation to Europe and East Asia. The problem for Africa is that without such capabilities there are few countervailing influences over the increasingly capital-intensive technologies imported from the West. What is required in this area, as most elsewhere in the developing world, is investment in technological effort

> to acquire, master, adapt and improve upon existing technologies. This effort is often quite significant. In fact, developing countries often have to undertake greater effort than their counterparts in advanced economies because their absorptive capacities are much lower. Absorbing technologies is not a trivial or costless task, and industrial success depends on how well the process is managed.
>
> (Lall, 2005:10–11)

Around the year 2000 there were several studies of technological capabilities in African manufacturing, and these painted a generally unflattering picture of what was occurring. Structural adjustment, for example, was seen as neglecting the whole issue, with its exclusive emphasis on prices and markets (Stewart et al., 1992). During the past ten years or so, however, the topic seems, like that of technical choice, to have all but disappeared from the literature. This is unfortunate, partly because technology in general has rarely been accorded serious attention in the region, and a lack of academic writing on it will hardly help to rectify the problem. It is also unfortunate because there is now little or no literature that addresses the possibilities raised by the new global system of innovation – that is, one that has become, much more than before, reliant on research conducted in ultra-large developing countries, such as China and India. This, in turn, raises the probability that new technologies will be more in line with developing rather than developed-country factor scarcities, prices and incomes (see more below in Chapter 6).

I turn, finally, to the supply-side of the labour market in Africa, where conditions generally serve only to underline the region's status as a limiting case. For, not only has population growth (of around 2.6 per annum) there long served as the world's highest, but also it shows no sign of slowing down. Consider, in this regard, the entries shown in Table 3.1, which are taken from a recent UN Report.

Compare, to be more specific, the annual average growth rate in the population between 2015 and the estimated level in 2050 across all the regions shown in the table. The results are presented in Table 3.2.

Thus, compared to the moderate rates of population growth predicted for Asia and Latin America (of 0.57 and 0.68 per cent), Africa will have to confront the implications of a much higher 3 per cent growth rate (and nothing short of a doubling of the population over the period). In terms of the figures from earlier in the chapter, one such implication is a pronounced elongation of the labour supply

Table 3.1 Population of the world and selected areas and years (in millions)

Area	2015	2030	2050	2100
World	7349	8501	9725	11213
Africa	1186	1679	2478	4387
Asia	4393	4923	5267	4889
Latin America and the Carribean	634	721	784	721

Source: UN, 2015:1.

Table 3.2 Average annual growth rates of population between 2015 and 2050, all regions

Region	Percentage change (annual average)
World	0.92
Africa	3.1
Asia	0.57
Latin America and the Caribbean	0.68

Source: Based on Table 3.1

curve ('more than half of global population growth between now and 2050 is expected to occur in Africa' [UN, 2015:3]). Note, too, 'A rapid population increase in Africa is anticipated even if there is a substantial reduction of fertility levels in the near future…. After 2050, Africa is expected to be the only major area still experiencing substantial population growth' (UN, 2015:3).

Note, finally, that I did no more than mention the size of the formal sector as a determinant of whether and how effectively structural change occurs. Yet, I do possess enough data to make a rough estimate of how fast the industrial sector might need to expand if it is merely to absorb the increase in the labour force; that is, even before any attempt is made to absorb the surplus labour in the informal sector of the typical African country.

We know, for example, that in such a country the formal sector does not constitute much more than 10 per cent of the population, say 10 out of 100 million people (it could just as well be 5 out of 50 or 1 out of 10 million). We also know that the labour force increases at around 3 per cent per annum (Fox et al., 2013), thus requiring the formal sector to grow in this case at 30 per cent just to absorb the increased workers. If some of those working in the informal sector are also to be incorporated into the modern sector, growth will need to be even higher than this percentage. Such numbers as these constitute, in my view, a relatively neglected but nonetheless crucial aspect of the lack of structural change in Africa. It means that an awful lot will be asked of the demand for labour in manufacturing industry,

Table 3.3 Estimated population in Africa

Millions	2015	2030	2050	2100
	1186	1679	2478	4387

Source: UN, 2015.

a demand which is heavily influenced by the choice of branch in the industry and the selection of technology within the selected branch.

Conclusions

As a prelude to the comparative analysis of manufacturing in Europe and East Asia on the one hand, and Africa on the other, this chapter began with a simple diagrammatic taxonomy, using both supply and demand dimensions of the Lewis model. In relation to the successful early and late industrialising countries of Europe and East Asia, emphasis was laid on the demand-side of the market and the largely neutral nature of technical progress, which resulted in a broadly constant capital-labour ratio as output expanded. Much attention was paid in those countries to local adaptations of new technologies. In Africa, by contrast, very little serious policy attention has been devoted to technology, technological capabilities or local adaptations of technology, against the background of a constantly rising capital to labour ratio, even among processes that used to be done best by manual methods. On the supply side, too, the working of the Lewis model has been and will continue to be compromised by an alarming rate of current and future population growth, which has the effect of creating a pronounced elongation of the labour supply curve. By 2050, for example, it is estimated that the population will have more than doubled compared to today's levels on the continent. When one adds to this the small relative size of the formal sector, the growth rate required just to absorb the increase in the labour force may be of the order of 30 per cent (see Table 3.3 for recent estimates of population growth to 2100).

Indeed, by the year 2050 it is predicted that Africa will be the only major region which is still experiencing rapid population growth.

Notes

1   This assumption has been questioned by those who point to conspicuous consumption out of profits by wealthy individuals and repatriation of profits by multinationals to their home counties.
2   The notion of an elongated supply curve of labour is due to Bloom & Freeman (1987), who discuss the connection between population growth and the increase in the labour force.
3   Note, as Lewis (1979) has remarked, that these calculations need to take into account both immigration and emigration. Thus, 'the expansion of the modern sector is not necessarily tied to the population of the traditional sector in the same country, since migrants may come from outside' (Lewis, 1979:219). Note further that none of the countries in Western Europe experienced a shortage of labour before 1914, with the exceptions of

France and Germany. 'In all the others the modern sector was not growing fast enough to absorb all the rural migrants. This situation changed after the second world war, when low population growth combined with rapid industrialisation to create a shortage of labour' (Lewis, 1979:219).

4   So unrelenting is the pace of mechanisation, that it has now even reached sewing, a process that has long resisted the automation process. In particular, a new robotic sewing machine is said to be threatening jobs in low-wage countries (*The Economist*, 2015b).

5   It is important to note in this context, 'During the 1960s, a transition to lower population growth took place in South Korea & Taiwan, thereby reducing the pressure to reduce employment over time' (Podeh & Winckler, 2004:267).

6   Golub & Hayat (2014) show that minimum wages in relation to GDP are much higher in most low-income countries in Africa relative to other regions, especially East Asia.

4 The (un)sustainability of Africa's growth path

The three previous chapters have attempted to show that African growth in the past few decades has not worked well in terms of the Lewis dual-economy model. Rather, the general pattern has been one with a heavy bias in favour of resource-dependence and capital-intensive technology. It has created un- and underemployment on a large scale (especially among the youth), as well as high levels of income and other forms of inequality and a persistent tendency to generate high levels of poverty (though there are of course exceptions to this general picture). This chapter speaks to the sustainability of the African model by asking whether and to what extent said poverty, inequality and underemployment are likely to engender crime and violence in the region.

I seek to answer this question specifically in relation to Africa, though crime and violence data there are somewhat sparse and often of questionable accuracy. Where necessary, therefore, I turn to alternative evidence of a more general kind, while recognising that it may have more limited relevance to the African experience. It is also necessary to recognise that the analysis is complex; for each variable – underemployment, poverty and inequality – that is to say, there are numerous possible crimes and different disciplinary approaches to understanding the mechanisms involved in each of them. I hope, nevertheless, to convince the reader that relationships of the expected kind can generally be discerned in the theoretical and empirical literature on the topic.

I begin the chapter with an outline of what is to come in the sections below. Thereafter, for the sake of convenience, I provide a summary of the features of underemployment, poverty and inequality that generally obtain in Africa (in some cases I have added to the descriptions of these variables from previous chapters).

Table 4.1 A summary of Chapter 4

1   Profiles of poverty, (youth) unemployment and inequality in Africa
2   Unemployment, underemployment and crime/violence
The economics approach and its limitations
Multidisciplinary and non-economic approaches
3   Inequality and crime
Tolerance to inequality (the 'tunnel effect')
Inequality and homicides
4   Poverty, crime and violence
5   Conclusions

Profiles of poverty, (youth) unemployment and inequality in Africa

Corresponding to this table, I begin the chapter with a brief summary of the major characteristics of poverty, (youth) unemployment and inequality in Africa. These are shown in Table 4.2 and at least in part, reflect the consequences of the development strategy pursued in the region (as described in earlier chapters).

The overall impression one gains from the table is that if there are links between the variables shown there and conflict, then Africa should suffer relatively from crime and violence, as far as most other developing countries go. The purpose of the rest of this chapter is to discuss the nature and intensity of any such links (though it needs to be emphasised at the outset that comparative data on crime and violence[1] in developing countries are somewhat scarce and more often than not, of dubious quality).

Table 4.2 Poverty, inequality and vulnerable employment in Africa

Dimension	Observations
Poverty	• The absolute number of poor has risen from 280 million in 1990 to 330 million in 2012 (Beegle et al., 2016). • 72% of youth population in Africa live on less than $2 a day. Incidence of poverty among youth in Nigeria, Ethiopia, Uganda, Zambia and Burundi is greater than 80%.
Inequality	• The predictable result of resource-centred dualistic, capital-intensive growth is a high degree of inequality. • For Africa, as a whole, the Gini ratio increased from 0.52% in 1993 to 0.56% in 2008 (Beegle et al., 2016). This figure is high by the standards of other developing countries. Of the 10 most unequal societies in the world, 7 are drawn from Southern Africa.
Vulnerable employment	• 'South Asia and Sub-Saharan Africa account for most of the vulnerable employment globally – for both it stood at over 75 per cent, in 2013 (projected to decline only slightly by 2019)' (ILO, 2015:2.7).
(Youth) unemployment	• 'Africa has the youngest population in the world. The number of young people in Africa will double by 2045' (Africa Economic Outlook, 2012). There have not been enough new jobs to accommodate the existing youthful labour force, not to speak of any forthcoming increases.
Open unemployment	• Rates are typically relatively low in much of Sub-Saharan Africa. They are not infrequently below levels in developed countries. The real problem in the region is underemployment rather than open unemployment.
Underemployment	• Underemployment is to be found mainly in the informal sector. This sector typically accounts for at least 80% of total employment and in some cases as much as 90–95% (Golub and Hayat, 2014).

Unemployment, underemployment and crime/violence

Although I extend the complexity of the division at a later stage, it is useful at the outset to consider economic versus non-economic approaches to crime and violence.

The economics approach

According to its best-known proponent, Gary Becker (1968), the economics approach is narrowly defined to eschew the need for other disciplines in understanding crime and violence.

> The idea is that would-be criminals rationally weigh up the expected costs and benefits of breaking the rules. If the probability of being caught or the level of fine is too low, then the expected costs might be outweighed by the benefits. In this case, crime does pay and crime can be rational. The same logic applies to much more minor rules.
>
> (*The Economist*, 2012)

It is perhaps useful in this regard to consider some illustrative numbers.[2] Take the case of price-fixing by cartels. Assume, to begin with, that these institutions are routinely able to overcharge by 20–30 per cent. Assume, further, that agencies of the state that police such behaviour apply sanctions of between 10 and 40 per cent. If, then, there is a 50 per cent detection rate, with sanctions varying between 10 and 40 per cent, the expected cost of price-fixing by cartels is in the 5 to 20 per cent range. But if instead one uses a 10 per cent detection rate, the expected costs of punishment fall to 1 to 4 per cent, the expected benefits outweigh the costs and the crime is committed (quite rationally from this choice perspective). The logic of the approach is taken to be quite versatile, applying, for example, to situations where the sanctions are much smaller (such as with traffic fines).

More relevant for our purposes, however, is an implication of the basic economics model that 'given the low opportunity cost of violence to the poor, they have a comparative advantage in violence. Those without access to legal, cooperative gainful employment were more likely to maximize their utility by recourse to violent conflict and extortion' (Cramer, 2012:3).

One of the best-known applications of this line of argument is the work by Collier (2000) and associates (Collier & Hoeffler, 2004) on the economics of civil war in developing countries. Basing itself partly on the share of the young in the population, their proposition was that a predominance of young males in a society with few legal earning opportunities 'would predispose that society to a high risk of civil war' (Cramer, 2012:3). Conversely, an increase of such opportunities, would, by increasing the opportunity cost of participation, reduce that risk. Note that in this and other economics-based contributions to the study of violence and civil wars, 'employment and unemployment are viewed in straightforward income terms, and implicitly labour is treated, in textbook fashion, as a commodity like any other' (Cramer, 2012:3).

Recalling, now, from Table 4.2 that Africa has the world's youngest population, one would expect on economic grounds, a relatively high incidence of civil wars in the region. Surprisingly, however, as Collier & Hoeffler (2004) have themselves discovered, this is not what has in fact occurred. In particular, over the period 1960–1999, they find that for the sample as a whole (comprising Africa and other developing countries),

> the incidence of civil war was about 6 per cent. The incidence of civil war starts in Africa was slightly higher at about 8 per cent. However, other developing countries also had an above-average incidence, of around 7 per cent. To summarise, these statistics show that Africa did not, on average over this forty-year period, experience a much higher level of war starts than other countries.
>
> (Collier & Hoeffler, 2004:6)

Quite ironically, however, the authors seek to salvage their economic model with arguments of a more sociological kind. For example, they point to widespread ethnic and religious diversity in Africa, which, in their view, tends to make societies safer.[3]

On the specific link between unemployment and violence, the economics approach relies, as noted above, on the opportunity-cost argument. Numerous writers in this tradition see unemployment as a direct cause of conflict and violence. Some supportive correlative evidence for this view has been provided by the World Bank (2011) as shown in Table 4.3.

The evidence, however, is not confined to Africa and it is also not clear what type of variables – economic or otherwise – actually drive the result.

In any case, much doubt has been cast on the theoretical and empirical aspects of the Becker-type approach to the relationship between un- and underemployment and violence. Few such criticisms, however, fail to recognise that economic variables usually play *some* role in an overall explanation. The point, rather, is that they comprise only a part of the whole story. Thus,

> Explanations for conflict based purely on economic motives are inadequate – to avoid violence, societies must do more than just create economic growth.

Table 4.3 Reasons for rebel and gang participation

Rebel participation	
Unemployment / idleness	39.5%
Feel more secure / powerful	15%
Belief in the cause / revenge / injustice	13%
Gang participation	
Unemployment / idleness	46%
Feel more secure / powerful	13%
Belief in the cause / revenge / injustice	8%

Source: World Development Report, 2011:80.

The attention in recent years to quantitative correlations between economic factors and conflict has led some to argue that economics is all that counts. Not only is this facile – it misrepresents the state of the research. It is much more difficult to test the importance of identity, ideology, injustice and political motivations using statistical methods, but current research suggests that these are very important in explaining violence and conflict.

(World Bank, 2011:81)

For example, there are several studies of Latin American and African gangs and rebel recruitments that reveal links between 'employment, respect and identity' (World Bank, 2011:79). Indeed, these studies form part of a larger literature on unemployment and domestic violence, which underlines how the use of power and perceptions of 'dignity' may be more salient than pure economic motives as causes of violence.

This is consistent with employment being more than a purely financial transaction. It is also a social interaction, carrying aspects of personal status and expectations of how one should be treated. In other words, the nature of work relationships on offer matters a great deal.

(World Bank, 2011:79)

Ethnographic research on Sierra Leone and elsewhere, for example, elicits the finding that 'oppressive work relations' appear to be a major cause of rebellion.

Other criticisms, however, go so far as to entirely neglect economic variables. And yet others argue that recognising labour markets as intrinsically social phenomena is inconsistent with the economics paradigm. Solow (1990), for example, views these markets as social organisations in a manner that ordinary goods markets are not. 'The principal reason for and example of this is that both employers and employees … incorporate in their institutional exchanges "social norms", and in particular norms of fairness and ideas of status' (Cramer, 2012:4).

Non-economic and multidisciplinary approaches

I have already alluded to several studies that combine economics and other disciplines. To these I now add a few more that relate specifically to Africa.

One of them has to do with the Ivory Coast and the set of factors that led to a civil war in the country, after the passing away of the president in 1993.[4] To some degree, the war was the result of persistent socio-economic inequalities between the northern and southern areas of the country. More specifically, the rebels in the disadvantaged northern areas explicitly mentioned two grievances. One had to with the relative economic depression in those areas and the other was about negative feelings engendered by an apparent lack of (sufficient) state recognition of Muslim religiosity. Bear in mind, though, that 'to portray identity as driven by economic considerations alone is to ignore the consistency with which the qualitative literature identifies such features as humiliation, pride, and desire for affiliation as motivators for action' (World Bank, 2011:82).

Similarly, Stewart's analysis of horizontal inequalities in Kenya supports a major result of research on such inequalities and conflict, namely, that 'it is where political as well as socio-economic HI's are present and in the same direction, with the same groups deprived in both economic and political terms, that violent political mobilization becomes more likely' (2010:149). Thus, for example, in the 2006–07 Kenyan cabinet, political and economic frustrations were both ignited. On the one hand, the cabinet failed to include certain major political groups, and on the other, it was these very same groups that were undergoing various socio-economic hardships. 'It was the prospect of this situation being sustained through perceived electoral fraud that was mainly responsible for the past election violence' (Stewart, 2010:150).

The final example refers to the ways in which lack of employment opportunities among males (and economic deprivation more generally), have led to an increase in domestic violence in Kenya and Tanzania (Silberschmidt, 2001). The causal nexus in both countries is that:

> Lack of access to income-earning opportunities has made men's role as heads of household and breadwinners a precarious one. With a majority of men bereft of its legitimizing activities and often reduced to 'figureheads of households', men's authority has come under threat and, most importantly, so has their identity and sense of self-esteem.
>
> (Silberschmidt, 2001:665)

Thus affected, men seemed to be 'yielding to an exaggerated "owner"/macho behavior and physical violence against women' (Silberschmidt, 2001:665). It is more than likely that this mechanism also applies to other countries in East Africa and indeed elsewhere in the region. After all, the absolute numbers of poor have, as shown above, increased over the recent past in Africa, and the challenge this poses to other patriarchal societies would seem to be a general one. Note, finally, that this mechanism applies as much to poverty as it does to un- and underemployment in the taxonomy provided in Table 4.2.

Inequality and crime

Partly because data about them have been specifically gathered and partly on account of their prevalence in Africa, I focus in this section on (inequality and) homicides.

Inequality and homicides

In a technical sense, inequality affects poverty, since, for any given growth rate, the degree of inequality influences the number of those living in poverty. In particular, the higher is the former for any given growth rate, the less positive will be the effect on the latter, and vice versa. But there are also more direct relationships between these variables, one of the most compelling of which is the frustration and anger among those who feel unfairly left behind in the competition for high-paying jobs and incomes. This is broadly referred to as 'strain theory' from the criminology literature, and I shall return to it below, after dealing with the patterns and causes of inequality in Africa and the incidence there of homicides (relying on data collected by the UNODC, the United Nations Office on Drugs and Crime).

Recall, to begin with, the entries in Table 4.2 which showed, on the one hand, that Africa is a relatively unequal region (with an average Gini coefficient of nearly 0.6), and, on the other, that out of the world's ten most unequal countries, seven emanate from this region. Such ultra-inegalitarian economies, moreover, are drawn mainly from Southern Africa. Much of the extreme equality in this region may be due to what has been referred to as 'grafted capitalism' (ILO, 2013:2).

> During colonization, that is to say, the capitalist sector of the economy was grafted onto a pre-capitalist form of production in a distorted manner. This kind of capitalism did not transform the economy as a whole, but only a small enclave sector, thus failing to produce growth and development. The small formal sector was totally dependent on external factors such as markets in, and capital from Europe.
>
> (ILO, 2013:2)

Moreover, because of minimum wage legislation, transnational firms and union activity, wages in the formal sector are usually much higher than a free market would dictate (thus further exacerbating the gap between modern and traditional sectors).

In Southern African and other resource-dependent countries in the region, inequality was severe even at the onset of the colonial period, and not much has changed since then. Extractive industries have continued to intensify inequality and poverty. They have underlined the enclave-like character of the extractive economy and the facilitative role played therein by the government and private sector. Thus, 'while oil, copper, gold, diamonds, chrome … are in plentiful supply in the SADC (Southern African Development Community) region, unemployment is increasing, poverty is deepening and inequality between and within countries is widening (Jauch, 2011:1).

Much of this dynamic can be attributed to political economy factors, such as the alliance between the state and the mineral enclave part of the economy. Also important are the overlapping interests of foreign and domestic capital, neither of which has an interest in fundamentally changing the status quo (Ross, 1999). Thus it is that in spite of all the rhetoric espoused in post-apartheid South Africa, the extent of inequality there remains exceptionally high.

What then is the impact of inequality on homicides? The UNODC concludes that 'inequality is also a driver of high levels of homicide. Homicide rates plotted against the Gini index … show that at global level, countries with large income disparities … have a homicide rate almost four times higher than more equal societies' (UNODC, 2011:30). This correlative evidence extends also to Africa, in the less affluent areas of which, one third of the world's homicides take place.

In per capita terms, as shown in Table 4.4, homicide rates in Africa are the highest in the world. More generally, the UNODC finds a clear correlation between the numbers of homicides and levels of development (a result that fits in the section below dealing with poverty and crime).

Table 4.4 Homicide rates per 100,000 population by region (2010 or latest available year)

Region	Homicide rate per 100,000
Africa	17.4
Americas	15.5
World	6.9
Oceania	3.5
Europe	3.5
Asia	3.1

Source: UNODC, 2011.

Thus, the homicide rate in Africa is more than 2.5 times higher (per capita) than the world average and nearly 6 times as high as the figure for Asia. Given what we know to be high relative inequality in the former region, these results contribute to the tendency at the global level for inequality to be correlated with homicides (as just noted).

But if there is such a tendency (the data used by UNODC are not of a level that allows for firm conclusions), what underlies it? I am drawn here to strain theory and especially its emphasis on anger and frustration.[5] What the theory posits is that

> strains, particularly major strains (store) that are seen as unjust, are likely to make individuals angry. This anger creates pressure for corrective action, interferes with the use of certain legitimate coping strategies, such as negotiation, reduces concern for the consequences of one's behaviour, and creates a desire for revenge. And data suggest that anger … partly explains the effect of strains on crime.
>
> (Agnew, 2012:36)

Interestingly, strain theory is quite versatile in the range of outcomes that it can help to explain. Thus, the theory

> also focuses on other negative emotions and certain recent research is exploring the idea that different types of strain lead to different negative emotions (e.g., anger versus fear), and that different emotions are conducive to different types of crime (e.g., anger to violence, depression to drug use).
>
> (Agnew, 2012:36)

A sense of injustice and anger at one's inability to earn a decent living, for example, are common causal features of the violence experienced in civil wars. They were also described above as being important to the gender violence that was committed in East Africa, when men's socio-economic status was (as noted above) severely threatened.

Tolerance to inequality as development proceeds

Rarely do all sectors of an economy or the socio-economic groups within it, progress equally as development proceeds. Inevitably, some of them will be left behind as change occurs. How they respond – whether with equanimity or anger – determines in part whether or not the outcome will be violent. And this in turn, as the tunnel effect explains, will depend on how the emerging inequality is perceived.

Assume, to begin with, that 'an individual's welfare at any point of time depends on both his present as well as expected future level of contentment … although the individual generally has good information about present income, his information about future income may be far more limited' (Ray, 1998:200).

Contemplate next an improvement in the situation of some of those around him. How the individual reacts to the new situation will depend on what it portends for his own welfare. He may, for instance, interpret the improved situation of the others as a favourable augury for his own prospects in the foreseeable future. In such a case, the welfare of the individual left behind will not be diminished by what has happened to those around him. On the contrary, he may well experience an enhanced sense of well-being as a result of it.

This somewhat paradoxical outcome implies that greater inequality will at the least be well tolerated on the part of the individual who is left behind. It is referred to by Hirschman and Rothschild (1973) as the 'tunnel effect' (after the analogy of a two-lane traffic jam where drivers in one lane are faced with progress by cars only in the other lane). Intolerance to the inequality thus generated, however, would tend to occur if the improved position of others is judged as irrelevant to the individual's own prospects. It might be the case, for example, that society is sharply divided among ethnic, racial and other dimensions. An improvement in the welfare of those from different ethnic and racial groups would then say little about the individual's future prospects.

'Such variations in the responses of individuals to a rise in the fortunes of others', writes Ray (1998:201) 'explain the differences in the tolerance of inequality, both across societies and over time'. Societies which are more differentiated in terms of race, ethnicity and so on, will tend to be more intolerant of growing inequality than more homogenous countries. For example, 'countries such as India or Pakistan might tend to have a much lower tolerance level for inequality compared to (relatively) more homogenous societies such as Mexico' (Ray, 1998:200).

Africa fits quite readily into this framework because it is one of the world's most ethnically and religiously fragmented regions. 'Africa's ethnic fractionalization is on average 61 and its religious fractionalization 51, which is much higher than the fractionalization indices of 34 and 30 measured outside the region' (Collier and Hoeffler, 2000:7). Thus, any future test of the tunnel effect should pay particular attention to the role of countries in the Africa region and their predicted intolerance to changes in inequality.

Table 4.2 indicated that poverty is still a major feature of most African countries. Indeed, 'Today the percentage of people living on less than $1.25 a day in sub-Saharan Africa (41 per cent) is more than twice as high as any other region (such as Southern

Asia, with 17 per cent)' (Pew Research, 2015). An obvious question is whether so pronounced a degree of poverty also contributes to crime and violence in the region.

Some such evidence, in fact, is contained in earlier examples from this chapter. Collier and Hoeffler's (2000) study of the determinants of civil war in 161 countries, for example, finds that income appears as a statistically significant explanatory variable (even when Africa is separated from the larger group). One of the reasons for this seems to be that higher income supports the government over the prospective rebels in a country and thus reduces the risk of war. The point is that 'higher levels of income are associated with differentially stronger government finance as the government takes a rising share of income as tax revenue' (Collier and Hoeffler, 2000:4). The converse would presumably apply to lower incomes (poverty).

The second study, of gender violence in East Africa, is more qualitative and sociological than the first, but it also lends credence to the notion that poverty begets violence. The argument, as Silberschmidt (2001) convincingly puts it, is that 'socio-economic change entailed by increasing poverty has perhaps been just as harsh for men as for women – but in a different and more obscure way. Men seem to have been submitted to a larger extent than women to new obligations and expectations and following this, new systems of social value'. More specifically,

> My data … clearly demonstrate that a majority of men are not able to honor their expected role as head of household and breadwinner. This has serious consequences for men's social value and it is a constant threat to their masculine pride. As a result, men have had to find new ways to manifest themselves… sexual manifestations and control over women – often acted out in violence and sexual aggressiveness – seem to have become fundamental to restore male self-esteem.
>
> (Silberschmidt, 2001:668)

Perhaps the most convincing general case for poverty as a harbinger of crime, however, has been made by Bourgignon (1999). Taking a distinctively economic approach to the matter, his view is that from this perspective, the major reasons for crime are either the appropriation of someone else's property, or the illegal pursuit of activities which run the risk of detection and punishment.

> Therefore, it is natural to expect that crime offenders be found among those who have relatively more to gain from these activities and relatively little to lose in case of being caught. These presumably belong to the neediest groups in society, their number being larger and their motivation being stronger the more unequal the distribution of resources in society.
>
> (Bourgignon, 1999:62)

To his credit, however, the author does not overstate the explanatory power of economic over other variables, such as those from sociology and criminology. Indeed, he believes that there are many circumstances in which such other variables explain more of the link between crime and poverty. In Brazilian favelas and other urban slums in developing countries (including Africa[6]), for example, the prevalence of poverty, drugs, gangs and gambling interact in complex and multifaceted ways to create and maintain high levels of crime (Jones and Rodgers, 2011).

Consider, finally, Bourgignon's reading of the then (1999) available, but limited, empirical evidence, which leads him to suggest that

> an increase in the degree of relative poverty … in a country generally leads to a rise in criminality, be it the actual crime rate or the propensity to commit crime in that part of the population not confined to prison. By increasing the extent of poverty, major recessions may have an effect of comparable amplitude on crime…. It follows that, through crime and violence, the social cost of inequality and crime may be large.
>
> (Bourgignon, 1999:95)

In fact, in such circumstances, social costs may run to as much as 2 or 3 per cent of the GDP.

Conclusions

This chapter has examined the consequences for crime and violence of the following features of the typical African development model, namely, that it is inegalitarian, dependent on relatively high rates of (youth) unemployment and involves high amounts of poverty by most other developing country standards. The results are difficult to summarise, however, for several reasons – one is that there are a host of different crimes ranging from burglary and thrift on the one hand to gang violence and civil wars on the other. Another is that there are a variety of different approaches to understanding each of these crimes, varying from the economic to the criminological and sociological. In this respect, several authors argue that the economic model fares better in relation to property crimes, whereas for homicides and civil wars, sociological variables tend to make more sense.[7] Most situations, however, seem to require a multidisciplinary approach.

I hope to have shown, nonetheless, that empirical studies – qualitative and quantitative – tend to confirm that the variables contained in Table 4.2 do indeed tend to incite crime and violence (some notable exceptions notwithstanding). To this extent, the generally prevailing development strategy in Africa seems to entail social costs[8] that are not normally taken into account by policymakers or other influential actors. As such, the sustainability of the prevailing model is not questioned frequently enough. Indeed, what needs to be recognised is that the crime and violence I have described may ultimately imperil the longevity of the growth rates among countries in the region.

Notes

1 See, for example, World Bank (2011), Cramer (2012) and UNODC (2011).
2 These numbers are taken from the *The Economist* (2012).
3 Though later in the chapter, an argument is set forth that ethnic fractionalisation in a society increases the chance of violence.
4 See World Bank (2011).
5 This theory is widely used in the criminology literature. See, for example, Agnew (2012).
6 See also the case study of Cape Town in UNODC (2011).
7 See Demombynes and Özler (2002).
8 For calculations of the size of these social costs, see Bourgignon (1999).

Part II

Countervailing tendencies and policies

5 Towards labour-intensity in African manufacturing

My argument thus far has been that the past and present strategy of African industrialisation has been and continues to be heavily lop-sided and generally unable to create enough jobs for a rapidly growing labour force. This is already manifest, I argued, in an acute problem of underemployment in the informal sector of the typical economy in the region. Nor does the future seem much more promising. For example, the World Bank (2013a) estimates that there will annually be 10 million entrants to the labour force in sub-Saharan Africa, all of whom, according to the Lewis model, need to be absorbed into the formal sector.

Such an estimate, as I see it, only amplifies what is already a dire need in Africa, namely, to radically alter the pattern of manufacturing in favour of increased labour-intensity. Indeed, so formidable is this task thought to be, that it needs to do more than alter the choice of technology, important though this topic surely is to any endeavour to create more jobs. What also needs urgent attention is the choice of manufacturing branch and the composition of units (i.e., the combination of large and small firms) within any given branch (the latter because firms of different size tend to adopt very different technologies).

The choice of manufacturing branches

Data compiled on the labour-intensity of numerous sub-sectors of manufacturing are shown in Table 5.1 for South Africa.

The table shows a marked variation in labour-intensities ranging from 62.64 for garments at the one extreme, to 1.71 for paper and paper products at the other. Notice that the former are more than 5 times as labour-intensive as textiles. That is, for every 1$ invested, 5 times as many jobs can be created in the one case as against the other. Note too that garments are also the highest-ranked branch when it comes to indirect employment effects, that is, the backward and forward linkages that connect specific sectors to one another (Tregenna, 2012).

With its remarkably high rate of open unemployment[1] and a clear focus in policy documents on employment creation, one might have expected South Africa to pay particular attention to garments and other labour-intensive branches of manufacturing. Yet, 'a striking feature since 1994 has been the continued rapid growth of resource based (and capital-intensive) industries. Growth in these sectors, and in

Table 5.1 Labour intensity, selected branches of manufacturing, South Africa (descending order)

Branch	Labour-capital ratio*
Clothing	62.64
Furniture	31.21
Footwear	27.53
Leather	18.47
Metal excl. machinery	11.86
Textiles	11.52
Wood & wood products	11.29
Plastic	11.23
Rubber products	4.84
Food	4.29
Beverages	2.93
Tobacco	2.73
Glass & glass products	2.29
Paper & paper products	1.71

Source: Tregenna, 2012.
*mean of 2006–2009, current prices.

the automotive industry, has far outstripped other sectors of manufacturing' (Black and Hasson, 2012:6).

Indeed, according to the same authors,

> South Africa's industrial policy has been fairly interventionist but in the wrong direction. It has acted to strengthen competitive advantage in resource-based, capital intensive sectors of manufacturing and undermined the prospects of more labour demanding sectors. Industrial policy needs to shift away from direct or indirect assistance to more capital intensive sectors and should be used to actively promote more labour demanding sectors and sub-sectors.
>
> (Black and Hasson, 2012:2)

Lest it be thought that such comparative neglect of light manufactures has been confined to South Africa, consider the entries in the following Table 5.2, which applies to Africa as a whole and shows the growth in the share of manufactures between 2000 and 2009.

Perhaps the most notable entries in the table are the slow growth of labour-intensive manufactures over the period, in comparison to the more capital and skill-intensive alternatives (that is, a growth of 1.6 compared to 5.7 per cent). Note, too, that contrary to what one might have expected, apparel does not feature prominently even in the former category, in spite of its exceptionally favourable labour-intensity.

Table 5.2 Growth in African manufactures (compound annual growth 2000–2009)

Branch	Growth rate (%)
Food & beverages	1.1
Paper	2.9
Rubber & plastic	4.1
Tobacco	1.6
Wood	-1.9
Fabricated metal	3
Textiles	0.9
Apparel	2.3
Publishing & printing	2.7
Furniture	3.2
Leather	0.8
Chemicals	8.4
Electrical machinery	5.9
Low technology	1.6
Medium high technology	5.7

Source: UNECA, 2014.

Not all African countries, however, have neglected the potential afforded by labour-intensive manufactures such as garments. Some of them, for example, have explicitly promoted these goods in the context of export processing zones (EPZs), which enjoy various fiscal and other benefits in designated areas.

Export processing zones (EPZs)

There was a rapid increase in EPZs in Africa during the 1990s and 2000s. Indeed, in 2011 Farole observed that there were then zones in 30 countries and that 80 per cent of them had been established during the 1990s and 2000s. Many of them have achieved little success, and not much is known about their experience. Moreover, even the literature on the relatively successful cases is somewhat out of date and unhelpful to policymakers in the region who need to be apprised of recent developments. What is known about these cases (Mauritius, Madagascar, Lesotho and Kenya), however, is that they have tended to specialise in garment manufacture. For each case, I have gathered data about employment in EPZs for selected years, as shown in Table 5.3.

Note that although the absolute amounts of employment created are not that high, the countries concerned are – with the exception of Kenya – relatively small. Thus, the per capita achievements are much more impressive, especially in Mauritius and Madagascar. If these same employment to population rates could be replicated in larger African countries, the numbers would run into the hundreds of thousands.

Table 5.3 Employment in EPZs, selected countries and years

	Date of establishment	Employment	Year
Mauritius	1970s	90,000	1991
Madagascar	1990s	100,000	2004
Kenya	1990s	39,111	2005
Lesotho	–	50,000	2004

Source: Baisser, 2011; Cling et al., 2007; Farole, 2011; Shakya, 2011; Vastveit, 2013.

Table 5.4 Costs and productivity of garments, selected countries (US$)

	Monthly wages in garments production, polo shirts (unskilled labour)	Labour productivity in garments production, number of polo shirts per worker, per day
China	237–296	18–35
Vietnam	78–130	8–14
Ethiopia	26–48	7–19
Tanzania	93–173	5–20

Source: Dinh et al., 2012.

To these examples should be added the emerging case of Ethiopia, which is mounting a concerted effort to use EPZs as a means of attracting foreign investment and increasing manufactured exports and domestic employment. Not only is the country said to be building four new industrial parks, but it also relies on a special zone exclusively for garments. Indeed, in the past two years a number of major European countries have begun to source garments from there (McKinsey & Co., 2015). This is partly a matter of external conditions: production costs are rising in China, the world's major supplier of light manufactures, and several major accidents have occurred in Bangladesh, another leading exporter.

But it is also partly or even largely a question of productivity and costs. Consider, for example, the data contained in Table 5.4.

From the first column, it is apparent that Ethiopia, which has no minimum wage, enjoys a considerable wage advantage over the other countries shown in the table (especially China). But comparative advantage depends on more than wage costs alone: it is also dependent on labour productivity, in this case, the number of polo shirts per worker per day. The second column shows that Ethiopian productivity is exceeded by China but equal to that in Vietnam and superior to Tanzania. Overall, though, the higher Chinese labour productivity is outweighed by the difference in wage costs, so that Ethiopia retains its comparative advantage in garments production.

For this and other reasons – such as infrastructural improvements; a proactive approach to foreign investors; stable low-cost electricity; and favourable treatment under the African Growth and Opportunity Act (AGOA) – Ethiopia is increasingly being spoken of as a potential 'garment-sourcing hub' (McKinsey & Co., 2015).

Indeed, according to a recent McKinsey survey of a large number of chief purchasing officers in the sector, this country, and to a lesser extent Kenya, were the most frequently mentioned out of all sub-Saharan countries. 'For the first time in our survey', the report concludes, 'African nations appear on the list of countries expected to play more important roles in apparel manufacturing. Ethiopia, notably, is seventh on the list' (McKinsey & Co., 2015:1).

If there are therefore conditions which have favoured and continue to favour employment creation in some EPZs in Africa, it is much less clear how these institutions can be made to benefit other countries in the region, to a more than marginal extent. Many and long are the lists of what specifically needs to be done,[2] and much can be learnt from the successful cases. I will confine myself, therefore, to a few, relatively general remarks.

The first is that with the exception of the countries already mentioned above, African economies have not focused their export-processing activities on garments, and there would seem to be much scope for expansion in this sub-sector, especially in the light of the developments in Asia, mentioned above. The second point is that the lagging countries have much to do before they reach even the level of the emerging cases, such as Ethiopia and Kenya. For example, take the crucial case of infrastructure and consider in particular the entries shown in Table 5.5.

The table shows average monthly downtime due to power outages in six African countries. It is clear that even to get down to the Kenyan level (of 11 hours), countries such as Nigeria and Senegal would have to make drastic improvements in the power they supply to their EPZs (getting down to Lesotho's level is an even more demanding requirement).

The third point is that even though this and other policy changes are formidable, one needs to recognise that they have typically not been pursued with much conviction until now in most African EPZs. On the contrary, Farole (2011) and others talk of a lack of commitment to these institutions in the region. In countries such as Lesotho and Kenya, on the other hand, policies seem to have been undertaken rapidly and with vigour. For example, 'when AGOA opportunities became available, Lesotho made stronger, clearer efforts to attract direct foreign investment than other countries in Southern Africa' (Shakya, 2011:228).

Table 5.5 Average monthly downtime due to power outages (hours) (special export zones)

Country	Hours
Ghana	34
Kenya	11
Lesotho	2
Nigeria	136
Senegal	67
Tanzania	50

Source: Farole, 2011.

The choice of techniques[3]

From the 1970s to the mid-1990s, there were a spate of studies on the choice of techniques in African industries.[4] Since then, though, there have been hardly any, for reasons that are not entirely clear. After all, it is not as if the issue itself has become less compelling than it was before. Indeed, it may now even be more important than before, as automation inexorably makes its presence felt.

The earlier literature did enough, however, to demonstrate that in much of African manufacturing, large-scale, capital- and import-intensive technologies tended to be favoured, even though efficient labour-intensive alternatives were generally available (as would be expected in poor, labour-abundant countries). In fact, so widespread was this tendency that one paper from that period went so far as to ask how many jobs in manufacturing would be created in a typical African country by a switch from inappropriate to appropriate technology (Pack, 1982). The data he used for nine branches of manufacturing are shown in Table 5.6.

More precisely, Pack uses market prices that are thought to typify most African countries, and, basing his calculations on various other assumptions, he compares for each of the nine branches shown in the table two technical alternatives, namely, the most capital-intensive and the one that is appropriate. The former 'may be thought of as a turnkey plant designed by a consulting engineering firm or, a diversified equipment producer' (Pack, 1982:6). The other technique can be described as the alternative, which maximises the present discounted value per unit of capital cost. Pack then proceeds to estimate, for each branch, the differences in value added, employment and capital per worker that would occur as a result of investing a given amount, $100 million, in the two techniques whose specifications have just been laid out. When they are aggregated over all the branches described in Table 5.6, Pack's results are shown in Table 5.7.

In the aggregate, therefore, the appropriate option is seen to involve not only a far greater number of workers but also a much greater degree of value added. If one assumes that all the manufacturing firms in the economy were, at the time, using the inappropriate alternatives, then the total difference in employment would have been equal to 180,661 (i.e., 238,678 − 58,017). This is admittedly an extreme assumption, one that would not fully hold in reality. On the other hand, though, the choice of technology in Africa is known to be biased in favour of modern, turnkey projects that are highly capital-intensive (as many studies have shown).[5] It seems reasonable to conclude therefore that the number just cited at least approximates what would happen to employment should firms shift from the inappropriate to the appropriate technology across manufacturing as a whole.

This conclusion, moreover, is likely to understate the true employment effect, because it ignores the indirect effects of the competing technology choices. If these effects were to be included, it is more than likely that the value added and employment increases estimated by Pack would be even more pronounced, since the appropriate technologies tend to be better integrated into the wider economy. Khan and Thorbecke (1989) found, for example, 'that the direct and indirect linkages generated by relatively labour-intensive techniques were in most cases appreciably greater

Table 5.6 Labour– versus capital-intensive techniques in manufacturing

Sector	Annual output of plant	Capital-intensive technology			Appropriate technology		
		Investment in thousands of dollars	Number of workers	Thousands of dollars per worker	Investment in thousands of dollars	Number of workers	Thousands of dollars per worker
Shoes	30,000 pair	334	155	2.2	165	218	0.8
Cotton weaving	40,00,000 sq. yards	9,779	260	37.6	4.715	544	8.7
Cotton spinning	2,000 tons	1,440	98	14.7	480	240	2.0
Brickmaking	16,000,000 bricks	3,437	75	45.8	796	238	3.3
Maize milling	36,000 tons	613	63	9.7	219	96	2.9
Sugar processing	50,000 tons	6,386	1,030	6.2	3,882	4,986	0.8
Beer brewing	200,000	4,512	246	18.3	2,809	233	12.1
Leather processing	600,000 hides	6,692	185	36.2	4,832	311	15.5
Fertiliser	528,000 tons of urea	34,132	248	137.6	29,597	242	122.3

Source: Pack, 1982; Table 1.

Table 5.7 Employment and output implications of two technologies at the macro level

Technique	Value added (\$ million per annum)	Employment (all workers)	Capital-labour ratio (\$ per worker)
Appropriate	624	238,678	3,771
Capital-intensive	364	58,017	15,513

Source: Pack, 1982; Table 3.

than those generated by the more modern, capital and import intensive alternatives' (James, 1995:25).

If, with these additional indirect increases in employment, the gains from switching to labour-intensive techniques seem considerable, so too do the barriers involved in achieving them (large enough at least to rival the costs involved in bringing about a successful EPZ, as described above). For one thing, as argued in Chapter 9, for every large-scale inappropriate plant there would have to be numerous smaller-scale ones. This might require organisational skills on a scale not seen before in the country (see Chapter 9). And if one is forced on this account to rely on the turnkey alternatives, there are engineering limits to the extent to which labour can be substituted for capital, even assuming, as seems unlikely, that such adaptive capabilities are available in the country (I have already referred to the deplorable state of technological capabilities in most African counties).[6]

In any case, large-scale projects often involve foreign (notably Western) consultants and machinery suppliers, whose preference for the latest vintages militates against the selection of older, more labour-intensive alternatives, especially in environments where pressure to reduce costs is not severe. James (1995), for example, reviewed a series of public-sector manufacturing ventures in East Africa and found little or no local input regarding the choice of technology. What appeared to be happening, instead, was that local bureaucrats were concerned with maximising the inflow of foreign (Western) finance for political reasons, and were hence very attracted to supplier's credits, aid and foreign investment. The resulting technology was simply the fallout from this essentially political process, especially the drive for political power that a large-sized, foreign-financed enterprise engendered. If the foreign finance happened to materialise in a particular country, so too did the technology. And since most of the finance emanated from the West, so too did the machinery and other major inputs.[7]

Since the time when these studies were undertaken in East Africa, however, a major change has occurred in the financial context of African manufacturing. And with it comes the hope of more appropriate technical choice in the sector. Foreign direct investment (FDI) is one source of such optimism: in particular, the rise in the share of direct investment that emanates from developing, rather than developed, countries. Data collected by a recent World Bank Report (2015a), for example, show the major investors for overall FDI and FDI in manufacturing for five selected African countries. They show in particular that while 'Traditional partners accounted for large stocks in 2012–2014 for overall FDI', they:

represent much less proportion in manufacturing FDI. In contrast, the bulk of FDI inflows to the manufacturing sector were from new partners and intraregional partners, led by China, India and South Africa. The major fields of investment are textile and clothing and leather and footwear; and motor vehicles and transport equipment for both India and China in manufacturing.

(World Bank, 2015a:16)

I have yet to explain, however, why this shift in the source of FDI might improve the choice of technology in African manufacturing. It has to do with the fact that China, India and Turkey all possess substantial capabilities to innovate in this area and indeed will have already developed technologies different from those in the West. In particular, the innovations will tend to be more labour-intensive (given the relative abundance there of this factor) and the products more appropriate (given the relatively low average incomes that prevail there). When managers of FDI from China, India and Turkey come to choose technology for their African projects, so the argument continues, they will be inclined to choose the alterative that is familiar to them and best suited to the conditions of the African countries in which they invest.

Unfortunately, no one has sought to test these propositions and more generally. 'Very little is known about the relative factor intensity of Chinese investment in SSA and its contribution to job creation' (Pigato and Tang, 2015:11).[8] This is clearly a major lacuna in the literature, which deserves to be filled as soon as possible. There is, however, some information about the factor intensity of foreign firms in Thailand, whose country of origin was also from the developing world (Lecraw, 1977). Such information was compared to data for other multinational and for domestic Thai firms.

The results are striking and very much in line with the hypothesis advanced in the previous paragraph. Specifically,

> Within each industry, LDC firms were on average 39 per cent less capital-intensive than either other foreign firms, or local firms....
> In general, LDC firms used technology which was appropriate to local factor costs whereas other foreign firms and local firms used 'inappropriate' technology....
> LDC firms, especially Indian firms, often used absolutely efficient technology.
>
> (Lecraw, 1977:453)

Underlying these results is a propensity for LDC firms to source their machinery from their host countries or from domestic Thai firms, as shown in Table 5.8.

Perhaps the most telling statistic in the table is that Indian firms source 45 per cent of their machinery from their host country and 25 per cent from local Thai firms (making a total of 70 per cent from developing rather than developed countries). For other LDC firms, the percentage spent on machinery from their home countries was 25 per cent, the same figure as for local purchases (making a total of 50 per cent bought from developing countries). On the other hand,

Table 5.8 Ownership of the firm and the country of origin of the machinery it used

Nationality of the firm	Country of origin of the machinery						
	US	Europe	Japan	India	Other LDC	Thailand	Percent (%)
US	51	25	16	0	0	8	100
Europe	20	57	13	0	0	10	100
Japan	6	4	80	0	0	10	100
India	4	10	8	45	8	25	100
Other LDC	7	8	30	5	25	25	100
Thailand	30	27	26	2	2	13	100

Source: Lecraw, 1977:454.

domestic firms sourced an overwhelming percentage of their machinery from developed countries.

Whether or not firms from China, India and Turkey will follow this predilection for home technology in African manufacturing remains to be seen. There is certainly no recent evidence one way or the other, though there are examples from the 1960s and 1970s in East Africa, which show Indian and Chinese firms engaging in relatively appropriate technical choices.[9]

Note, finally, that although I have dealt only with FDI, the same basic argument also applies to aid from developing countries to Africa, and especially the recent growth in Chinese aid. In the case of tied aid, for example, there is a direct link to Chinese technology and the characteristics that are thought to be associated with it. But although it is growing rapidly,[10] such finance to Africa is still a long way off from Western levels. So, any macro effect on employment from more appropriate technology will be limited correspondingly.

Composition of units

As noted above, the composition of units refers to the share of investment going to actors differentiated by size, ownership and so on.[11] It is important to note that there is nothing sacrosanct about the existing composition in any given country. Indeed, many authors have pointed, for example, to the widespread biases in developing countries against small-scale firms, which are typically much more labour-intensive than their large-scale counterparts. Some of the biases derive from government allocation decisions (regarding, say, infrastructure or foreign exchange). Others are due to market imperfections of one kind or another (that is, deviations from the state of perfect competition).

Finance is worth singling out as an area of resource allocation, because it is replete with imperfections that favour large- over small-scale firms. The recent experience of Ethiopia well illustrates the point. Thus, according to a World Bank Report (2015d) on manufacturing in the country, 'young and small firms are the most likely to report that access to finance is a major constraint to their business operations' (Geiger & Moller, 2015:35). Specifically, '40 percent of small firms, and 18.5 percent of medium firms reported access to finance to be a major constraint to daily operations' (Geiger & Moller, 2015:35). Much of the problem, it seems, has to do with the fact that

> young and smaller firms are much more likely to be rejected for a loan or a line of credit than firms who are more established or larger .... Moreover, despite confirming their need for improved access to finance, SMEs are discouraged from applying for loans due to excessively high collateral requirements. Only 1.9 per cent of small firms have a loan or line of credit.
>
> (Geiger & Moller, 2015:35–36)

Finally, demanding collateral requirements constitute a binding constraint on small-scale firms, because the most typical type of collateral is land, buildings or personal assets. 'As elsewhere in developing economies, Ethiopian banks prefer immovable collateral such as land rather than movable assets such as machinery. Large firms are the only ones who can use equipment as collateral' (Geiger & Moller, 2015:36).

In order to counteract these and other biases that work in the same direction, Stewart et al. (1992) call for 'structured markets.' By this they mean

> reserving a proportion of resources—credit, foreign exchange and so on – for the small-scale sector and thus ensuring that a 'market' solution generates adequate resources for the sector. Structured markets of this kind were successful in securing resources for the small-scale sector in India, where the requirement that 1 per cent of credit be allocated by the major banks to the small-scale led *inter alia* to the establishment of the Self-employed Women's Association.
>
> (Stewart et al., 1992:26)[12]

Moreover, since some of the biases against small-scale are due to public allocations (of funds, foreign exchange to technology, infrastructure), structured markets should be applied in these institutions as well. And in some cases, institutions that cater directly to the needs of micro and small enterprises will need to be established. One can think, here, for example, of appropriate technology institutions and micro-finance organisations such as the Grameen Bank.[13]

An especially promising idea in this regard is to combine EPZs with particular support for SMEs, as has been done to great effect in some of China's 'plug-&-play' centres. According to the World Bank,

> These industrial zones played a critical role in facilitating the growth of Chinese SMEs from family operations catering to the local market to global powerhouses. These zones not only provided Chinese SMEs with good basic infrastructure (e.g. roads, energy, water and sewage), security, streamlined government regulations (e.g. government service centres) and affordable industrial land, they also provided technical training, low cost standardized factory shells allowing Chinese entrepreneurs to 'Plug and Play' as well as Chinese workers

with free and decent housing accommodations right next to the plants. Hence they played a very critical role in helping Chinese small enterprises to grow into mid-size and large enterprises.

(Geiger & Moller, 2015:48)

The attractiveness of this model for African and other countries has largely to do with its being able to structure all kinds of markets in a single location where the effects can be combined rather than dispersed across different government institutions. 'In a nutshell, the Chinese government facilitated SME development through the efficient provision of public goods and market information about sellers and providers but not subsidies .... Most importantly, competition between firms is intense. The government does not bail out failing firms' (Geiger & Moller, 2015:48).

The final theme that I wish to raise under this heading turns on the difference between indiscriminate and targeted assistance to SMEs. This distinction would of course hardly matter if SMEs tended to be very similar to one another, as is sometimes thought. Recently, however, Diao et al. (2016) have found a striking degree of heterogeneity among small-scale firms (from manufacturing and service sectors) in Tanzania, on the basis of an unusually rich data-set.[14] Some of them, the more dynamic ones, exhibit relatively high labour productivity – indeed, a small group of such firms, comprising just 10 per cent of the total, enjoys annual average labour productivity that is '80 per cent higher than average economy-wide productivity in manufacturing' (Diao et al., 2016:1). They also show that 'this small group of informal firms has the potential to contribute up to 1.3 percentage points to annual labour productivity growth' (Diao et al., 2016:1).

On the problem of being able to actually identify and promote these more promising firms, the authors discuss broadly two alternatives. One has to do with competitions of various kinds. In Nigeria, for example, the government instituted a national business plan competition in 2011 which cost around 36 million dollars. Out of the 24,000 applicants, 1,204 were ultimately successful and were each granted an amount of roughly 50,000 dollars. An evaluation of the winners, three years after they had received their awards, showed that they were more likely to survive and had indeed grown into firms with at least 10 workers.[15] (This does raise the question, though, of whether a lesser amount, granted to more applicants, might have yielded an even better outcome.) More recently, in Tanzania, a competition for young entrepreneurs has been proposed, which is designed to elicit promising young (ages 18 to 30) entrepreneurs who are already in business. 'Winners of the competition will be supported along three dimensions: finance, access to networks and mentorship' (Diao et al., 2016:32). Business competitions, though, have not been invariably successful and in some of them, it is not clear what the outcome actually was.[16] More research is needed here in order to discern why some such endeavours are successful and others less so.

Given the unusual degree of firm-level detail that their data-set contains, Diao et al. (2016) also consider using the discriminant (observable) features of the firms they identify as promising. Noting the difficulties associated with identifying firms with potential from observable features, they nonetheless feel that 'it seems worthwhile to use the very rich dataset we have to understand better whether or not we can identify any differences in observable characteristics that might be used for reaching out to high potential firms' (2016:33). It is not surprising, though none-theless interesting, that the small group of promising firms they identify shares cer-tain key features with formal sector enterprises, to wit, that their owners are more educated, that they use more modern technologies and that they are substantially more likely to do business with modern banking institutions.

Conclusions

African development strategy over the years has rarely engaged itself in a serious way with employment creation in the manufacturing sector (notwithstanding the rhetoric on the subject that so frequently appears in government policy papers). This chapter, accordingly, has suggested three main areas in which the situation might be redressed. In particular, I have dealt with (1) altering the choice of manu-facturing branch in favour of those that are especially labour-intensive; (2) changing the choice of technique within any branch in the same direction; and (3) changing the composition of units in any chosen branch, towards appropriate – technology-using small-scale firms with the potential to grow in terms of employment and productivity.

In each case, there appears to be considerable scope for employment creation in countries which sorely need it in order to absorb a rapidly growing labour force. But I have also emphasised the severe difficulties involved in making the necessary alterations in practice (on the choice of technology, moreover, an entire chapter is still to follow on the difficulties wrought by the close link between scale and factor intensity). What makes these difficulties severe, one should emphasise, is not just economic constraints but also those that are more political in character.[17]

At the same time, however, there is a pressing need to intensify the efforts being made in the neglected dimensions I have suggested. For, as emphasised in Chapter 4, the status quo of growing poverty, inequality and underemployment may at some point conspire to threaten the social fabric of African societies.

Notes

1 In 2014, for example, youth unemployment in the country was greater than 50 per cent (World Bank, indicators).
2 See, for example, Dinh et al. (2012) & Farole (2011).
3 Although I have conceptually sought to distinguish between them, the choice of sector and the choice of technique are in fact connected. This is because even at the level of say, garments, there is not one but many technical choices at different stages of the manu-facturing process. The point is that each such stage tends to have its own factor intensity: basic cutting and sewing, for example, are relatively labour-intensive stages of garment making. This allows these stages to be carried out in the developing countries, while the more capital- and skill-intensive processes are conducted in the rich countries. Indeed, it is precisely this kind of distinction that allows labour-abundant countries to form part of supply chains in certain manufactured goods.
4 See, for example, the studies reviewed in Stewart et al. (1992), James (1995) and Stewart (1977). The first two of these citations deal specifically with Africa, whereas the third deals with developing countries more generally.

5 See the research described in the previous footnote.
6 See, for detailed information, Lall and Pietrobelli (2002).
7 In this sense, it is inaccurate to speak of a choice of techniques. It would be more accurate to speak of a choice of project.
8 What is known is that between 2003 and 2014, Chinese foreign investment in African manufacturing created nearly 40,000 jobs (through 77 projects). See Pigato and Tang (2015).
9 See James (1995).
10 See Sun (2014).
11 The term is due to Stewart (1987).
12 The Indian case can, however, be criticised as being indiscriminate. See Diao et al. (2016).
13 See Stewart (1987).
14 Among other things the sample is representative.
15 See Diao et al. (2016).
16 Diao et al. (2016) refer to World Bank competitions in this regard.
17 Often, for example, vested interests grow up around capital and foreign-exchange intensive technologies, making it difficult to switch to more appropriate alternatives. See Stewart (1987) and James (1995).

6 The new global economic order

Prospects for African manufacturing

At the time when Lewis made his seminal contributions to the analysis of the dual economy (in 1954 and 1979), the world economic order was dominated by the rich countries. I use the term 'economic order' here to describe global R&D, trade, FDI and aid, though there are other dimensions that could be discussed (such as membership of international bodies). Since that time, across all the areas that have been mentioned, there has been a quite striking rise in the share of developing countries, especially, but not only, China and India. The purpose of this chapter is to describe how these changes will affect the future prospects for industrialisation in Africa. The main line of argument expressed across mechanisms of R&D, trade, FDI and aid, is that the increased participation of developing countries potentially imparts a favourable influence over manufacturing in the region, a few notable exceptions notwithstanding. Broadly, this is because developing countries such as China and India tend to share African problems and circumstances to a greater extent than the industrialised countries, and the solutions to those problems thus tend also to be more relevant. Note that these issues could hardly have been foreseen by Lewis in 1954, who, anyway, largely assumed a closed-economy model.

R&D

Indeed, one of the most salient mechanisms through which the new economic order affects Africa is that its innovations are increasingly being supplied by 'emerging' rather than 'traditional' partners. About 40 years ago, for example, only 2 per cent of global R&D was concentrated in the poor countries, and not even all of that was focused on the problems of such countries. By 2010, the relevant figure had grown to 20 per cent and is now almost certainly even higher.

What I expect from this global realignment is that more attention would have been paid to low- (and medium-) as opposed to high-income country problems, and that the resulting innovations in manufacturing would have benefited most consumers and producers in Africa[1] (though there may also be certain negative effects, which will be described below). This expectation, one should note, applies with special force to China and India, which have extensive R&D programmes even by developed country standards. (National Science Board, 2014). Let me begin though, with a few examples from the latter country, while noting that they represent only a small fraction of the many cases that could be cited.

The importance of the Indian pharmaceutical industry in this regard is best appreciated against a backdrop where

> [m]edicines account for 20–60% of health spending in developing and transitional countries, compared with 18% in countries of the Organisation for Economic Co-operation and Development. Up to 90% of the population in developing countries purchase medicines through out-of-pocket payments, making medicines the largest family expenditure item after food. As a result, medicines are unaffordable for large sections of the global population and are a major burden on government budgets.
>
> (Cameron et al., 2009:1)

India's medicinal drug industry fits well into this story because of its research into and supply of low-cost, generic drugs to developing countries as a whole and Africa in particular. For example, according to one estimate, almost 80 per cent of retrovirals in Africa are made in India (Waning et al., 2010). More generally, it is said that this country supplies almost 18 per cent of all pharmaceutical products to the region (SciDevNet, 2015).

The second example is narrower in scope but well illustrates nonetheless the main theme of how similarities in stages of development across countries lead to similarities in preferences. I am referring here to the popularity in Africa of automobiles designed for Indian conditions.[2] In particular, at least three automobiles that are designed and manufactured in that Asian nation are proving to be attractive in at least one African country, South Africa (one of them is the Toyota Etios, the cheapest product that the company sells worldwide).

For China, I have selected off-grid lighting products, partly because of that country's prominence in the sector and partly because of the probable future salience of these products in Africa and elsewhere in poor, developing countries. One specific example is the partnership between China and Kenya over the establishment of a solid-state lighting technology transfer centre, which, as its name suggests, aims to train and strengthen local capacity in the area.[3] A related goal is to assemble and manufacture solar and LED products in Kenya itself.

Global trade

The most striking alteration in Africa's trade pattern over the past 40 or so years has been its increased involvement with China.

> Trade flows between China and SSA [Sub-Saharan Africa] have expanded rapidly during the last decade. In 2012 the total value of China-SSA trade reached US$ 160 billion, the result of an annual growth rate of 26.2 percent since 1995. China now represents more than 20 percent of SSA's total trade, up dramatically from just 2.3 percent in 1995.
>
> (Pigato & Gourdon, 2014:6)

On the exports side, Chinese growth has mainly increased the demand for Africa's natural resources, while, as regards imports, African producers and consumers have broadly benefited from the relatively low prices of Chinese goods, as reflected, for example, in an average disparity with local producer prices of around 50 per cent (see Table 6.1 on this for a selected sample of manufactured goods).

These sizeable price differences, however, reflect disparate influences which need to be separated out, as they have varying welfare effects. Part of the disparity, for example, may reflect the simplicity of the products that are in demand by relatively low-income consumers and producers in China. I have described this earlier in terms of an appropriate balance between functional and inessential characteristics (the distinction between branded and generic drugs described earlier captures the idea). The design aspect of appropriate products may be bolstered moreover by lower costs of inputs and labour in China as compared to Africa (although the Ethiopian case shows that this is not invariably true).

Both of these aspects are illustrated in Figure 6.1, which contains two products, X and Y, and two characteristics, functional and nonfunctional.

Y is assumed to be the Chinese good and X the local African product. The former is relatively intensive in functional characteristics compared to the latter. And because of lower costs of production, one can purchase a relatively large amount of Y, yielding more of both characteristics than X (technically, the former is said to 'dominate' the latter, because the consumer or producer is better off, regardless of his or her preferences).[4] The corresponding amounts of characteristics are OB and OP versus OA and OQ, respectively.

The concept of appropriate products should not, however, be confused with another reason for the strikingly low price of Chinese imports to Africa, namely, the inferior level (or quality) of the essential characteristics embodied in them. Indeed, what I am now referring to can be more aptly described as another form of *inappropriateness*. For, it is not about an inordinate balance of inessential to functional characteristics – the original definition of inappropriate products. It is rather about a product that would *not* have been chosen if the buyer had full knowledge about the extent of each characteristic embodied in what we are assuming to be two competing goods, one domestic, and one foreign. More specifically, it is a problem

Table 6.1 Disparity of selected Chinese import prices with locally produced goods in Africa

Sector	Price gap in percentages
Beverages and tobacco	40–50
Footwear	70–80
Machinery	Approx. 70
Paper	50–60
Textiles and clothing	60–70
Wood products	40–50

Source: Pigato and Tang, 2015:8.

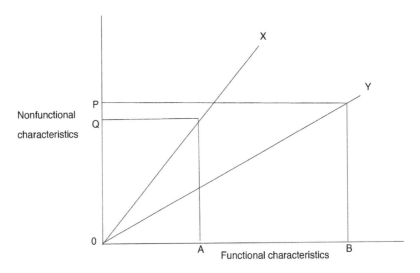

Figure 6.1 The basic diagram.
Source: Based on Lancaster, 1966.

caused by an overstatement of the true extent of the functional characteristic (say, durability) contained in the imported good.

In Figure 6.2, for example, X and Y represent, as before, the local good and the Chinese alternative, respectively. In the initial situation, the latter is thought to contain OR functional and OS inessential characteristics, while the corresponding amounts for good X are OQ and OT (at points A and B, respectively). Good Y is chosen because it leaves the buyer on a higher indifference curve than good X. In reality, however, the former contains only, say, OP of functional characteristics and would not have been selected had the buyer been fully informed (since point C offers less of both characteristics than point A). Again, the one good is said to dominate the other.[5]

Perhaps the most obvious example of this type of situation arises in conjunction with counterfeit Chinese imports, which purport to contain more characteristics than they actually do. For example, watches work for only a limited amount of time, while with garments the colours may run after only a few washes. In neither of these cases, one should note, could the true functionality be ascertained prior to purchase. Aside from counterfeits, Chinese imports may simply fail to deliver an adequate amount of functional characteristics, as was the case in Nigeria, where 'authorities are trying to stamp out subpar Chinese electric goods. Imported power strips and wiring have inadequate copper to handle Nigeria's 240-volt system' (*The New York Times*, 2014). It has been alleged that this problem was responsible for numerous electrically induced fires in the country.[6]

Such examples as these, however, will persist in Africa without some product standards, which most countries in the region sorely lack. But this does not mean that the chosen standards should merely replicate those found in the developed

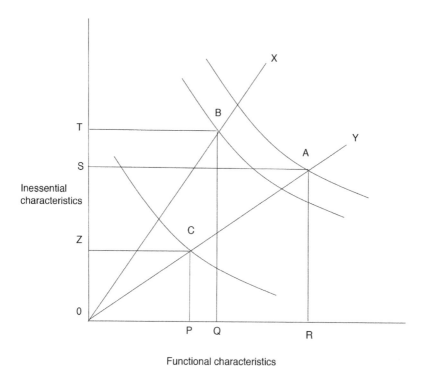

Figure 6.2 Counterfeit imports.

countries.[7] Demands for safety, for instance, depend partly on income levels: low-income buyers will tend to evaluate safety in a different way compared to those with average incomes in developed countries.

> By way of an (all too common) example consider the situation of a head of a low-income household in an LDC [less-developed country] who is taken ill and is unable to work. Deprived of any sickness benefit he is aware that even a relatively short period of loss of earnings can mean severe physiological hardships for himself and his family. In this situation he will almost certainly have a marginal valuation of the safety, efficacy and price of drugs which differs sharply from that implied by DC [developed-country] standards.
>
> (James, 1982:263)

What are needed can best be described as intermediate standards, which lie somewhere between no standards and developed-country levels, for essentially the same reason as one needs intermediate (appropriate) products and technologies (so far, however, most international policymakers seem intent on framing standards at developed-country levels, which tend to penalise those with low incomes in developing countries).

Displacement of local goods

Even if they are not subject to quality lapses of these kinds, imported Chinese goods may nevertheless give rise to acute problems of output and employment in competing domestic markets. Indeed, one African country study after another recounts the loss in local employment due to competition from Chinese (and other) imports.[8] Unfortunately, most such accounts of this phenomenon tend to be anecdotal. Edwards and Jenkins (2013), however, have used decomposition and econometric techniques to analyse the effects on output, employment and prices of these goods in manufacturing in South Africa.

Before I report their findings, though, consider Table 6.2, which shows the share of Chinese goods in total South African imports for selected manufacturing branches in 1995 and 2010. Most entries show a substantial rate of growth between the two periods. Indeed, by the latter year, products such as clothing and footwear had come to dominate South African imports. Moreover,

> Chinese penetration of the South African market is shown to have increased rapidly over the past decade, in part due to displacement of imports from other countries, but more importantly at the expense of local production. Exports of manufactures to China did not add significantly to industrial growth in South Africa, whereas labour-intensive industries were particularly badly affected by Chinese imports implying that the negative impact on employment was more than proportional to the output displacement.

Table 6.2 Share of Chinese products in total South African imports, selected branches of manufacturing

Manufacturing branch	1995 (%)	2010 (%)
Spinning and weaving	6.4	43.5
Clothing	29.0	75.1
Leather and leather products	10.2	49.0
Footwear	35.5	76.8
Furniture	2.4	48.1
Glass and glass products	3.1	38.6
Rubber products	0.5	23.1
Household appliances	13.7	62.6
Electric lamps and lighting	9.4	59.9
Paper and paper products	0.2	8.6

Source: Edwards & Jenkins, 2013:7.

However, we also find evidence that Chinese imports contributed towards lower producer price inflation in South Africa, which in turn will have moderated increases in consumer prices and helped to curtail production cost increases.

(Edwards and Jenkins, 2013:1)

It is difficult to overstate the significance of these findings in the context of a dual-economy model of development. For, in that context, the industrial sector already has the task of absorbing not just increments to the labour force – which are substantial in Africa – but also those living in the informal sector. As I have already argued, this is itself a formidable task. If, in addition, employment in manufacturing is on balance reduced by trade with China, the task becomes that much more challenging.

FDI

In terms of FDI to Africa, the most striking aspect of the new economic order is the rise of China. Thus, according to a recent World Bank report, 'China's FDI into Africa is significant and rising.' Between 2003 and 2012, 'direct investment flows from China to Africa grew at an annualised compound rate of 47.8 per cent, with investment stock increasing 52.5 per cent. In 2013, FDI from China is estimated at $3.5 billion, and cumulative investment stock at over $25 billion' (World Bank, 2015a:1). Note, moreover, that 'Chinese FDI to Africa is shifting towards the manufacturing sector…. As of the end of 2011, China's cumulative investment stock in the manufacturing sector in Africa grew year-on-year to $2.4 billion, and in 2013, it accounted for 15 per cent of Chinese FDI' (World Bank, 2015a:1).

Part of that investment will have gone into an attempt to re-create in Africa a model of industrialisation which has seen considerable success in China, namely, one that is based on EPZs (sometimes referred to as industrial clusters). It is represented in the former region, at arguably its most impressive, in an Ethiopian EPZ, by the Huajian Shoe Company, which employs 4,000 workers and has ambitious plans for the future.

On the whole, though, as Pigato & Tang (2015) point out, African firms have not generally been able to insert themselves into Chinese value chains. This 'limits the impact of Chinese investment on economic transformation and export diversification in SSA' (Pigato & Tang, 2015:4). Among the reasons they offer for this disappointing result are the small size of many African economies, the limited capacity of crucial public institutions, infrastructural bottlenecks, and the lack of regional integration.

More promising, according to Pigato & Tang, may be the rise of Chinese private investment in Africa, which they call nothing less than 'spectacular' (Pigato & Tang, 2015:17). Thus, for example, in 2002 only 4 of the 21 recorded Chinese FDI projects in Africa were privately owned, but by 2013 that number had risen to 1,217 out of 2,282 projects, or 53 per cent of the total (Pigato & Tang, 2015). No less than with its publicly led counterparts, however, data on the impact of Chinese private investment generally leave much to be desired. Once again, therefore, much remains to be researched if the potential future role of China in African industrialisation is to be realistically established. There is nonetheless some such information available from a case study of Tanzania.[9]

It shows, first of all, that that country has seen a rising share of the private component of Chinese FDI. For example, between 2002 and 2013, the number of Chinese private firms in Tanzania rose from 30 to around 300. Such firms, moreover, appear to have created anywhere between 80,000 and 150,000 jobs, an estimated range which compares very favourably with the roughly 15,000 jobs created by the country's EPZ authority. Note too that 'many Chinese firms provide on-the-job training to local workers and some also send Tanzanian managerial staff to China for training programs lasting from three months to one year' (Pigato & Tang, 2015:18). Most important, however, is the finding that, 'Most Chinese private firms are involved in low-tech, labor-intensive industries, such as light manufacturing and assembly, and many compete with domestic companies in Tanzania' (Pigato & Tang, 2015:17). To the extent that they actually displace such companies, therefore, the resulting losses in employment need to be offset against the jobs they create.

Equally recently, Shen (2015) has also described the small-scale, labour-intensive nature of Chinese private foreign investment in Africa, but he has also gone a step further. In particular, he has likened this form of investment to that which originates in other emerging economies such as India and South Africa. At least in its private form, therefore, Chinese foreign investment appears to differ from the large-scale, capital-intensive investment that is usually forthcoming from the developed countries. It is an area that well bears further scrutiny as a source of appropriate technology and jobs in African industrialisation.

Even more deserving of further study is the fundamental question raised by Ozawa (2015), of whether China will provide enough low-cost jobs in manufacturing to Africa to enable the region to take off, by effecting the rapid transformational kind of industrialisation that has occurred in parts of Asia.

Consider first in this regard the entries in Table 6.3, which show the extent of Chinese FDI to Africa as compared with some prominent developed and emerging economies.

Thus, the Chinese stock in 2012, though substantial, was equal to only about one-sixth of the three developed countries (though it does comprise about 40 per cent of the BRICs' FDI stock in that year). Note, moreover, that of the total Chinese stock in 2012, only 15 per cent went to the manufacturing sector (Ozawa, 2015) and of that some fraction would have gone to light manufacturing. Apart perhaps from Ethiopia, this last amount has not, however, brought about any obvious increase in (light) industrialisation in Africa.

Whether things will change for the better in the future depends, in part, on the willingness of the Chinese 'to decisively discard low-wage manufacturing in light industries by promptly transplanting it outside the country' (Ozawa, 2015:16). On the one hand, 'there is a newly crafted strategy of promoting manufacturing investments, especially by China's state-owned or state-backed large companies that the Chinese government controls – hence, can mobilize for policy purposes'

Table 6.3 The extent of Chinese FDI to Africa as compared with some prominent developed and emerging economies

Country grouping	FDI stock in 2012 in Africa
US, UK, France	$178.2 billion
China	$27.7 billion
BRICs (other than China)	$40.0 billion
Total BRICs	$67.7 billion

Source: Ozawa, 2015.

(Ozawa, 2015:13). There have also been, as noted above, a series of sharp wage increases in light manufacturing in recent years, which will work in the same direction of stimulating Chinese FDI to parts of Africa and other low-cost areas. On the other hand, as some authors have pointed out, there is still a very large surplus of labour in rural China, which will tend to have the opposite effect. Indeed, according to one view, 'China's rural labor reservoir will not dry up so quickly but rather remain to exist for quite a while' (Ozawa, 2015:17).

Partly for this reason, Chinese FDI alone is unlikely to be enough to bring about the type of structural change that is envisaged in the Lewis model. More investment from other countries will almost certainly be needed, but so far such resources have not been adequate to the task, not least because, on the whole, developed countries no longer engage in the type of foreign investment that Africa requires. More, perhaps, may be expected from the other BRICs, whose foreign investment in Africa, as noted in Table 6.3, collectively exceeds that of China and whose pattern of industrial production is arguably more in line with African requirements.[10]

Foreign aid

In the granting of aid to Africa, no less than with the other mechanisms that have been described in this chapter, developing countries (most notably China and India) have increased their presence. Thus, in the Chinese case, the amount of cumulative aid between 1949 and the end of 2009 was 43 billion US$, on the basis of the exchange rate prevailing in the latter year; whereas between 2010 and 2012, the amount was of the order of 15 billion US$ (Sun, 2014). 'This means that more than a quarter of the aid provided by China from 1949 to 2012 happened during the last three years of that period' (Sun, 2014). Indeed according to a Chinese white paper on the issue, Africa became the dominant regional component of that country's aid between 2010 and 2012 (Sun, 2014).

Although Chinese aid to Africa remains relatively small compared to the amounts provided by the OECD countries (Berthelemy, 2011), one might nevertheless have expected some research on the ability of that country's aid to promote industrialisation and employment in the region. This would have required, at a minimum, an estimate of the amount of aid that goes to the manufacturing sector, the choice of branch within that sector, and the choice of technology in the branch selected. Yet, as far as I can tell, no solid evidence exists on any of these issues (save for a couple of Chinese-aid financed projects in the 1960s and 1970s in Tanzania). There is thus no current basis for comparing the outcome of Chinese aid with aid from developed countries, with Chinese FDI or with local African firms.

What is clear, however, is that 'tied aid' will play a large part in any future research agenda. For, on the one hand, tying is an obviously important influence on the choice of technology; on the other hand, much Chinese (and indeed Western) aid is in fact tied.

> For example, if the government of an African country seeks a loan for an infrastructure project, that loan will typically come from one of China's two state policy banks, the China Exim Bank and China Development Bank. The banks are export promotion enterprises rather than development assistance agencies. Furthermore, contracts between African governments and Chinese policy banks typically stipulate preferential treatment for Chinese contractors and goods.
>
> (Hanauer & Morris, 2014)

The Exim Bank, for example, stipulates that at least 50 per cent of total procurements be made in China.

As I have suggested previously, Chinese technology may be generally more appropriate to Africa than technology from the developed countries at the specific branch level, so the fact that its aid is tied need not in itself be a major cause for concern (depending, of course, on its precise terms). Much will depend on the vintage of the chosen technology, since China may also produce large-scale, capital-intensive technological vintages for its aid-financed projects. In practice, it may be that the choice of scale determines the type of technology rather than the other way round, since projects rarely begin with technological choices. If so, one will need to investigate what factors in the early stages of a project determine its size. One of them will surely be the choice of manufacturing branch, since it may well be that appropriate technologies can be profitably used only in light manufacturing.

More generally, though, a major lesson of the existing literature on development aid is that if appropriate technology is to be promoted, it should happen at an early stage of the project cycle. Thus, to quote Jéquier & Hu,

> The appraisal stage is the only phase where one usually finds a discussion of the project's technological features. By that time, however, the project is so far advanced, and so close to a final decision, that no fundamental modification of its technical parameters can be made. Moreover, although appraisal reports usually describe the technical and engineering features of the project, the approach chosen is seldom compared with other possible alternatives, or justified in terms of such comparisons.
>
> (Jéquier & Hu, 1989:82)

Thus it is that the decisive technological influences are imparted at the identification and implementation stages rather than when the project is appraised. Yet, it appears that the appraisal stage is the one that receives the most attention in development banks in developing countries (Jéquier & Hu, 1989).

If this description is still valid – and there is no reason to think otherwise – it implies that governments in Africa will need to become more proactive in their dealings with Chinese (and other) aid donors. They will need to show a much greater degree of concern for technology, at a much earlier stage of the project cycle. Whether, and to what extent, this is happening is an important topic for research, as is a review of the appropriateness of Chinese aid in Africa.

Conclusions

Writing in 1954 and again in 1979, Lewis could not have anticipated the changes brought about in the international economic order by the rise in influence of the developing countries, especially China and India. This chapter has sought to examine some of the implications of this new order for the pattern and extent of industrialisation in Africa. In particular, I have studied four mechanisms through which the changes will have been implemented, namely, R&D, trade, FDI and aid.

My expectation in each case was that the new order would transmit a generally favourable set of impulses to Africa, since developing countries tend to have a greater affinity with the needs and preferences of the region as regards goods and technologies, compared with developed countries. Particular attention was paid to China, since that country has grown the most in terms of its influence on Africa, and it also has probably the most experience with the goods and technologies that the region needs. Table 6.4 presents a summary of the mechanisms envisaged by this hypothesis.

Table 6.4 A summary of the mechanisms

	Mechanism	*Examples*
R&D	China and India conduct R&D on poor country problems and come up with poor country solutions.	Indian pharmaceuticals and Chinese solar energy
Trade	China and India sell appropriate products and technologies to Africa, raising consumer and producer surpluses.	50% price gap between Chinese products and locally produced goods in Africa
FDI	China invests in relatively small-scale and labour-intensive branches of manufacturing and labour-intensive choices within each branch.	Chinese private FDI
AID	Aid donors and equipment suppliers in China sell technologies they are familiar with.	Certain forms of tied aid.

While there was some evidence supporting the said hypotheses, it was not sufficient to draw firm conclusions, and there were also a few notable exceptions which reduced the welfare of those involved. One such case, for example, concerns counterfeits and low-quality products from China that negatively affect the welfare of African consumers. Then, on the production side, there is the sometimes widespread displacement by cheap Chinese goods of local firms (though, of course, there will tend to be offsetting gains to African consumers of such goods).

My conclusion – albeit one of a distinctly speculative character – is that it will take a very substantial increase of Chinese and other BRIC resources to radically alter the existing pattern of African industry. Moreover, such an increase seems unlikely to be forthcoming in the foreseeable future, with the possible exception of Ethiopia. And if it is to occur, it will require, on the part of Africa, at least the same intensity with which that country has gone about attracting Chinese and other foreign resources.

Notes

1 Except, of course, for the top income deciles in those countries which identify more with developed-country problems and solutions.
2 This theme is closely related to the Burenstam Linder (1961) model of international trade, which emphasises the scope for trade between countries with similar incomes, as well as the fact that countries with similar incomes are likely to share similar preferences. Many arguments in this book have an affinity with this view. (Also see Stewart, 1977.)
3 See the *Nairobi Digest*, 28 July 2012.
4 I have chosen this case for simplicity's sake. But what really matters is that the consumer be on a higher indifference curve with Y than X, even if the latter offers more than one characteristic.
5 Dominance means that the one good offers more of *both* characteristics than the other.
6 See *The New York Times*, 2014.
7 For a full discussion, see James, 1982.
8 See, for example, Edwards and Jenkins, 2013.
9 See Ozawa (2015) for a discussion of this idea.
10 These cases are discussed in James (1995). In one of them, a textile plant, a comparison was made with a plant using what, at the time, were the most modern and automated technologies imported from Western Europe. Not surprisingly, the Chinese enterprise was much more efficient across a range of indicators. Though these examples are too few for many more general conclusions to be drawn, they are at least consistent with what has been suggested in this chapter.

7 A note on services as a growth escalator in Africa

One of the responses to the disappointing experience with manufacturing in many African countries has been to look for alternative sectors as growth escalators in the region. Of these, the most compelling is services, especially the Indian experience with this sector, which has relied not just on traditional activities, but also, and more importantly, on IT-related products (such as business process outsourcing (BPO) and call centres).[1] The question that this chapter seeks to answer is not so much whether services will allow growth to continue at the current pace (of around 2 per cent per annum per capita),[2] but more so whether they can help to increase that pace to the blistering levels achieved by the successful East Asian countries. It will be seen that because the data required to assess these questions are generally inadequate, the answers to them tend to be tentative and speculative, rather than well grounded and definitive. I begin though with the general case for services as a growth escalator in Africa.

The case for IT and services and its weaknesses

The most elaborate case in favour of a redirection away from manufacturing has been made by Ghani & O'Connell (2014). They offer three related observations in support of their case. The first is that the traditional mode of growth through manufacturing has become more difficult over time. In particular,

> Technological changes have made manufacturing more capital and skill intensive. So, it is creating fewer jobs, some form of pre-mature deindustrialization seems to have set in.... This might be because consumers and households in developed countries now spend a lot less on manufactured goods than they do on services. This can put a limit to how fast the latecomers to development can grow through industrialization. But there is no such limit in services.
>
> (Ghani & O'Connell, 2014)

It is of course generally true that the relentless drive towards automation over time creates less employment per unit of capital. But the jobs that were described above as being suitable for further advances in manufacturing (such as stitching and cutting in garments) are precisely those that are most resistant towards this tendency. Otherwise, in fact, there would be no foreign investment in this and other labour-intensive manufacturing branches in Africa. Yet, we have seen that this is clearly not the case.

Then again, as far as the supposed limits to industrialisation are concerned, the question for African countries is not so much the size of the total market for manufactures, as it is whether they can capture the share of it that is currently being made available by the move away from some labour-intensive products in China.[3] Even a small share of that vacated source of demand would constitute a very large number of jobs for countries such as Ethiopia, Kenya and Lesotho.

The second proposition advanced by Ghani & O'Connell (2014) is that services nowadays include not just traditional activities such as retailing, but also those based on IT. Thus,

> technology, trade and supply chains have altered the characteristics of services. Innovations in communication and transport have contributed to global supply chains being extended into parts and components of manufactured goods.... The core of the argument is that as the services produced and traded across the world expand with globalization, the possibilities for low income countries to develop based on their comparative advantage expand.
>
> (Ghani & O'Connell, 2014)

This argument would have been more convincing, however, had the authors described the particular mechanisms through which IT and services are related and explained how different African countries are thought to have earned a comparative advantage in them.[4] If it is thought to have been through BPO, for example, it would have been well to note how the experience in this area in two of the countries with arguably the most commitment to IT in Africa, namely, Kenya and Rwanda, fell well short of expectations. In particular,

> The local BPO sectors do not have the depth, scale efficiencies, cost-competitiveness and skill base to compete for international customers with established foreign BPO companies and markets. Due to a lack of international competitiveness, Rwandan and Kenyan BPO enterprises have largely expanded within their home countries or across Africa
>
> (Mann et al., 2015:4)

Ghani & O'Connell (2014) would also have done well to mention a simpler form of relationship between IT and services, namely, the creation of 'mobile money' in Kenya and certain other East African countries such as Tanzania. Known as m-PESA, the idea of using mobile phones for informal banking was introduced in Kenya in 2007, by Safaricom, a subsidiary of the British multinational, Vodafone. Briefly stated,[5] m-PESA amounts to 'an electronic payment and store of value system' that is made available by mobile phones. To gain access to the system, users must first be registered at a designated m-PESA outlet. There 'they are assigned a personal electronic money account that is linked to their phone number and accessible through a SIM card-resident application on the mobile phone' (James,

2016:44). Clients can deposit in, and withdraw money from, their accounts 'by exchanging cash for electronic value at a network of retail stores (often referred to as agents). Once customers have money on their accounts, they can use their phones to transfer funds to other m-PESA users and even to non-registered users, pay bills and purchase mobile airtime credit' (James, 2016:44). So successful has been this scheme, that it has reached over 60 per cent of the Kenyan population, employing at least 40,000 agents.[6]

The third observation made by Ghani and O'Connell (2014) is that, apart from China, services have expanded more rapidly in Africa and other countries than have manufactures. Consider in this regard the entries shown in Table 7.1.

From the first two rows it is clear that in both non-oil- and oil-producing countries in Africa, services have grown more rapidly than in manufactures, though in the case of the latter the difference is minute. Note, too, that nowhere in the region is the growth of services anywhere near what the East Asian countries achieved in manufacturing. There are, that is to say, few signs that the globalisation of this sector has created an opportunity for African countries to 'find niches, beyond manufacturing, where they can specialize, scale up and achieve explosive growth, just like the East Asian tigers did in manufacturing' (Ghani & O'Connell, 2014:3).

More fundamentally, however, the problem is that the authors confuse what is and what ought to be. The fact that services contribute more to GDP growth than manufactures is a positive not a normative statement. It may well say more about the relative policy neglect of manufacturing than about the strength of services. After all, I have been at pains to show how manufacturing in Africa has not been taken very seriously at the actual policy level, as distinct from the recommendations made in planning and other documents of the state.

And there *are* examples of countries in the region where a concerted push in the direction of EPZs in highly labour-intensive branches of manufacturing has, or seems about to, achieve notable results in terms of exports and employment. I am referring here not only to garments in Ethiopia but also to Kenya and Lesotho,

Table 7.1 GDP growth by sector, 1990–2012, selected regions and countries

Country/region	% growth in manufacturing	% growth in services	% growth in agriculture
Sub-Saharan Africa (non-oil producers)	3.2	4.2	2.2
Sub-Saharan Africa (oil producers)	2.8	2.9	2.5
Ethiopia	6.7	8.3	4.6
India	6.9	8.3	3.0
China	12.4	10.9	4.0
Low-income	2.1	3.2	2.5

Source: Ghani & O'Connell, 2014:9.

which are showing promise in this sector. Recall, moreover, the striking success of Mauritius and Madagascar in the export of these (and other) manufactured products in the previous century. All the relevant evidence on this is contained in a report by Dinh et al. (2012), which makes a persuasive case for light manufactures as a growth escalator in Africa, subject, however, to numerous constraints.

In some cases, moreover, policy failures towards manufacturing have been accompanied by encouragements to services. For example,

> In India and Sri Lanka, restrictive labour laws have hamstrung the emergence of a more competitive manufacturing base. In contrast India helped its information-technology sector by declaring it an essential industry and lifting the prohibition on operating around the clock in some states. In South Asia services have benefited from investment in telecoms infrastructure, as measured by the number of phone lines and personal computers per 100 people, whereas manufacturing is held back by a shortage of paved roads.
>
> (*The Economist*, 2011:2)

In Africa, as well, it is not difficult to find similar policy asymmetries. One only has to think, for example, of the massive expenditure on undersea cables for the provision of the Internet to East and West Africa, as against the limited amount of infrastructure (such as electricity) supplied to EPZs in the region (Ethiopia comes to mind, however, as a possible exception to this tendency). In many of these cases, therefore, the observed sectoral outcomes are not necessarily the ones that should be followed. Rather, they are the result of a particular (and not necessarily desirable) combination of differential sectoral support levels. The assumptions underlying them need to be closely scrutinised. As part of this process, we need also to consider the role of skills and jobs.

Skills and jobs

Ghani and O'Connell (2014) make much of the fact that in at least one African country, Ethiopia, labour productivity in certain service activities exceeds that of manufacturing. The details are shown in Table 7.2.

Table 7.2 Labour productivity per sector in 2011 Ethiopia

Sector	Labour productivity (thousands of birr per worker)
Agriculture	8
Manufacturing	17.8
Trade	29.5
Other services	36.7
Transport & communication	95.1

Source: Martins, 2014.

Leaving aside the positive versus normative distinction that has just been raised in relation to growth contributions and which also applies to productivity differentials, these findings are distinctly double-edged:

> The flip side of their high productivity is that modern services employ relatively few people. Just 2m of India's population of 1.2 billion work in information technology; in the rest of South Asia, only 100,000 do. That is one reason why India is still keen to promote manufacturing, which is also booming.
>
> (*The Economist*, 2011:2)

In addition to the paucity of the jobs they usually create, IT-based services also suffer from requiring a relatively skilled labour force. In South Asia, for example, workers in modern services generally obtain between one and three more years of education than workers in industry. Moreover, in such services, 'school grades or a university degree are often necessary' (*The Economist*, 2011:2). And in Africa, as distinct from India and certain other South Asian countries, it is precisely these demanding skill levels that are least in evidence. (Note in this regard the fortuitous fact that India's most prominent software exporters benefited from engineers who were trained in America and returned home to apply their knowledge. Note also the 'prevalence of English speakers' who were able to purvey their wares in American markets.... Many other developing countries lack these advantages' (*The Economist*, 2011:3).

Indeed, in the African context, I would argue that the vast majority of countries lack these particular advantages. Not only do few software engineers get trained abroad, but those that do tend to remain there. Moreover, it is only a minority of countries in the region that are English-speaking, and even fewer with language skills that can be described as 'neutral'[7].

Rodrik strikes a similar tone in addressing the question posed in the title of his 2014 article, namely, whether an African growth miracle is possible. He is sceptical of a major advance based on services, firstly, because of the lack of historical precedents for it – 'With few exceptions', that is, services traditionally have not acted as an escalator like manufacturing' (Rodrik, 2014:13). But the problems run deeper than this and manifest themselves most acutely 'in the fact that those services that have the capacity to act as productivity escalators tend to require relatively high skills' (Rodrik, 2014:13). The pre-eminent case in this regard is information technology, since 'Long years of education and institution building are required before farm workers can be transformed into programmers or even call center operators' (Rodrik, 2014:13). This requirement stands in stark contrast to that in manufacturing, 'where little more than manual dexterity is required to turn a farmer into a production worker in garments or shoes, raising his/her productivity by a factor of two or three' (Rodrik, 2014:13).

On the basis of the arguments that were adduced in the last few paragraphs, neither the *The Economist* (2011) nor Rodrik (2014) seem to feel that a growth miracle based on services is in the offing for Africa. The former, for example, concludes that for many countries, 'the conventional wisdom is still right: manufacturing holds the most promise for millions of reasonably well-paying jobs' (*The Economist*, 2011:3). For his part, Rodrik speculates that the current growth rate in Africa – of around

2 per cent per capita per annum – is sustainable, subject to the absence of major external changes, but for levels much beyond this, a growth model is required that is quite 'different from earlier miracles based on industrialization' (Rodrik, 2014). However, 'the balance of the evidence I have reviewed here suggests caution on the prospects for high growth in Africa' (Rodrik, 2014:14).

Conclusions

This short chapter has taken on the idea that modern services based on IT can be the source of a growth miracle in Africa. The claim is bolstered by evidence that services already contribute more to growth in the region than manufacturing (although it is largely unclear how much of the growth in the former is based specifically on IT). In any case, my main response to this evidence is that it confuses the positive with the normative aspects of policymaking. The fact that services currently outstrip manufacturing does not mean in itself that this is the most desirable state of affairs. In some cases, for example, the former sector has been encouraged by policy, while at the same time the latter has tended to be unduly neglected (I have in earlier chapters for example, alluded to the comparative neglect of a labour-intensive form of manufacturing). The outcome of such uneven policy is by no means necessarily desirable. It is not as if, for example, the past and present dominance of services in Africa has produced anything like a growth miracle in the region. In fact, for this to happen, a level of skills well beyond what is currently available would be required, since, as several observers have pointed out, modern services tend to be highly demanding of this resource, and most countries in the region are notably short of it.

However, as Rodrik (2014) has pointed out, the future may nevertheless look very different from the present. 'Perhaps', he suggests,

> Africa will be the breeding ground of new technologies that will revolutionize services for broad masses, and do so in a way that creates high-wage jobs for all. Perhaps. But it is too early to be confident about the likelihood of this scenario.
> (2014:13)

Notes

1   On the Indian experience, see Eichengreen & Gupta (2011).
2   See Rodrick's (2014) opinion below.
3   This has been discussed above.
4   It is not at all clear how African countries with few IT skills would generate a comparative advantage in modern services.
5   The following discussion draws on James (2016).
6   See *The Economist* (2013).
7   E.g. with accents that do not sharply deviate from the US norm.

8 Is there a renewed role for appropriate technology in the new global economic order?

In an article entitled 'Schumacher meets Schumpeter: Appropriate Technology below the Radar', Kaplinsky (2011) argues that the last few decades have witnessed a fundamental change in the global innovation system (as reflected, most tellingly, by a substantially increased share of R&D undertaken by developing countries, especially China and India). To this change should be added a massive increase in the incomes of the poor in the same two countries. These changes are integrated by the author into a framework of induced innovation, which predicts a new and vastly increased role for appropriate technology in developing countries, most especially China and India (where this type of technology is defined essentially as being relatively labour-intensive and associated with the type of product characteristics in demand by the poor). A separate chapter has discussed the possible impact of the new technology in Africa, a region where the role of China is especially pronounced (Chapter 6).

The purpose of this chapter is to question the assumptions made by Kaplinsky and to challenge the inevitability of the process he describes. In these respects I submit the following propositions: that he mis-characterises the situation with regard to appropriate technology in the 1970s and in particular wrongly assumes that the appropriate innovations in that period were made only by NGOs (thereby ignoring that already in that period appropriate technology was being widely used in certain developing countries; that he wrongly assumes that the absolute poor have no propensity to consume 'luxury'-intensive products, thus incorrectly excluding this group from the analysis; that he has no reservations about the induced innovation model; and that he ignores the relationship between appropriate technology and inequality (thereby ruling out for example the possibility that the thriving middle class in China and India may gain more than the income groups below it on the income scale). In the following three sections I shall deal with all these criticisms but I begin with an overview of Kaplinsky's argument and the assumptions that underlie it. The chapter seeks to provide more examples than Kaplinsky does, but there is far from enough evidence to arrive at any firm conclusions. Future research directions are suggested in the conclusions.

Outline of the argument

Appropriate technologies are defined by the Kaplinsky 'as technologies which are appropriate for low income countries in that they are labour-intensive, simple to operate and repair, producing products for low-income consumers at small scales and with a minimally-harmful impact on the environment' (2011:195). This type of technology is seen as undergoing a significant change that mirrors and is indeed the result of rapid recent growth of China and India. From being a concern only to NGOs in the 1970s and '80s, this type of technology, so the argument goes, has become and will continue to be 'an arena for profitable production' for private firms. (Note that in the early period low-income markets were generally not attractive to innovations designed for the high-income markets of the developed countries.)

The change thus described is seen as being caused by factors on the demand and supply sides of the market. As regards the former, the author points to the phenomenal reduction in absolute poverty in both China and India and more specifically to the 'very rapid growth in the number of people living in households with an annual income above $ 1,000 and less than $ 5,000' (2011:199). This, I should emphasise, entirely excludes those in absolute poverty, a point of contention to which I return below. On the supply side, a major feature of the new world innovatory order is the rise in the share of global R&D represented by developing countries, especially China. From a share of about 10 per cent of global R&D in 1990, developing countries had more than doubled that amount in just ten years (Kaplinsky, 2011).

The induced innovation model on which Kaplinsky relies incorporates both sides of the market, as recognised by Hayami and Ruttan (1987):

> Over the last several decades, advances in economic theory and the accumulation of empirical evidence have tended to confirm that the rate and direction of technical change can be interpreted as largely endogenous to the economic system – as induced by differences or changes in the conditions of factor supply and product demand. ...In the dynamic process of economic development, changes in product demand and relative factor prices are inseparably related.
>
> (Hayami & Ruttan,1987:58)

Hayami and Ruttan do not, however, conceive of technical change as being entirely induced by economic forces: 'In addition to the effects of change (or differences) in resource endowments and growth in demand, technical change may occur in response to autonomous advances in scientific knowledge' (1987:59). In such a case there is no way of knowing what the direction of technical change will actually be.

Kaplinsky predicts that the outcome of the induced innovation model in countries such as India and China will be (and some supportive evidence already exists) the use of labour-intensive techniques producing goods with an abundance of low-income characteristics such as functionality (as, say, in a detergent's cleaning ability as opposed to its scent and packaging).[1] Kaplinsky correctly asserts that the analysis of product characteristics can be conducted with Lancaster's framework, but he is wrong in claiming that this author applies his model to developing countries.

At no point in fact does Lancaster even refer to these countries. The connection was made instead by Stewart (1977) and James and Stewart (1981).

The predicted outcome stands in sharp contrast to the situation prevailing in the 1970s and '80s, when the global innovation system was based almost entirely on R&D conducted in and for the developed countries and demand by the poor for low-income products was limited by their income levels. This change, however, takes place 'under the radar' partly because there are so few contemporary studies of appropriate technology in China, India and Africa and partly because those that do exist do not delve into the product characteristics of goods in demand by the poor and other income groups (see more below on this).

The situation in the 1970s

Part of the reason why Kaplinsky envisages a 'significant' change in the role of appropriate technology between the 1970s and the present is that he mis-characterises the former period, describing it as a time when this type of technology was produced almost entirely by NGOs. Thus,

> Schumpeter's call for the development of AT influenced only a small audience, predominantly comprising of NGOs and some bilateral aid agencies. Reflecting Schumacher's own concerns.... It was essentially an ethical response to the prevalence of poverty rather than being driven by the pursuit of growth through the development (and use) of more profitable choices of technology.
>
> (Kaplinsky, 2011:195)

What Kaplinsky neglects, however, is the widespread production (and use) of appropriate technology for private profit in certain East Asian countries during the initial period. Also neglected are certain cases where this technology had a major impact, even in countries where the environment for the successful working of the induced innovation mechanism was far from propitious. With regard first to the newly industrialising countries of East Asia, consider first Amsden's description of the machine tool industry in Taiwan. Thus, beginning in a disequilibrium situation where costs exceed the average income of individual consuming units,

> Both costs and prices may be lowered, however, to reach an equilibrium by two procedures. Both involve producing a good not strictly comparable [to the good produced by developed countries] either in quality or complexity but designed to serve its same general purpose. Firms may in theory produce a simpler model or a miniaturized version of the [developed country product] (eq. a straight stitch rather than a zigzag sewing machine; a low rather than high hp tiller). As [the] product is qualitatively transformed, costs and prices may be hypothesized to fall until supply and demand are equilibrated. Not all goods, however, can be miniaturized or simplified. In such cases, a second alternative presents itself for lowering costs.... Such a sleight-of-hand may be accomplished by producing a poorer quality good .... by means of less modern, complicated and costly

techniques than a good of standard quality would necessitate. Such was the path followed by the Taiwanese machine tool industry. ... A less elaborate division of labour in the production of a lower quality machine tool also suited the factor endowments prevailing in Taiwan at the time.

(Amsden, 1977:219)

Similarly, 'in South Korea, after the mid-60s, examples of capital-stretching adaptations of imported technology abound in textiles, electronics, and plywood production' (Ranis, 1973: 402). As a result of innovations in these and other industries, it was possible for Korea actually to reduce the capital/labor ratio in manufacturing as a whole for part of the period after 1964; in Japan as well, the relative constancy of this ratio in the last part of the nineteenth century 'indicates the effectiveness of capital stretching innovations at the aggregate level' (Ranis, 1973:402).

In South Korea, finally, Pack (1981) shows how much of the impetus towards labour-using innovations in the textile industry came from the pressure to reduce costs for the export market (in contrast to India, where there was at the time limited pressure to do so).[2]

Even in India, moreover, there have been some impressive examples of labour-using technologies (including appropriate products) during the 1970s and 1980s. Probably the best known of them (and an exceptionally clear example of appropriate technology) was produced by a single Indian entrepreneur for the local market. His product, Nirma, was able to effect significant reductions on both the supply and demand sides of the production process. These, indeed, by the end of the 1980s,

> enabled the product to be sold at less than half the price of an equivalent amount of 'Surf', the then leading high-income laundry detergent. Indeed, at that same time 'Nirma' was barely more expensive than crude cottage-made soap cakes or loose detergent ingredients (which are sold in neighbourhood bazaars to be hand-mixed by housewives at home...).

> One means by which cost reductions of this magnitude were achieved lies in the realm of product design and in particular the design of a detergent specifically for low rather than high-income consumers. Thus, in contrast to 'Surf' and other brands designed to fit in with developed country conditions, 'Nirma' does not contain characteristics such as optical whiteners and scents, or ingredients designed to reduce the harshness of the product on hands and fabrics. Packaging, too, is an area in which there are important differences that bear on the costs of producing 'Nirma' as opposed to the competing high-income products. Whereas, for example, the latter brands are packaged in heavy cardboard, on which there is also sophisticated and expensive printing, 'Nirma' is sold instead in simple plastic bags on which the printing is relatively crude and hence much less costly.

(James, 2000:115–116)

On the supply side, the process chosen to produce Nirma further lowered the price at which it could be sold. 'In particular, this product is mass produced not by a single large factory but rather by means of a large chain or agglomeration of small workshops in which "people mixed the ingredients of washing powder by hand" (James, 2000:116).

So popular was the Indian product that it was able to capture the dominant share of the local market for detergents (and in the process stole much of that market from competing multinational firms). Note that Nirma's success was achieved in a sector where labour can relatively easily be substituted for capital. In other sectors (such as oil refining), this may be difficult or impossible.[3]

Note too that the concept of appropriate products is not only – or even mainly – about sacrificing quality in exchange for cost reductions. It is also importantly about the balance of 'luxury' and 'functional' characteristics.

The conclusion of this section is thus, that, contrary to what is claimed by Kaplinsky, appropriate technology produced by privately owned firms enjoyed a vibrant existence in at least some (and possibly more) developing countries in the starting period of my analysis. Consequently, if such technology has appeared in China and India since then, it is not as much of a novelty as he suggests. There are, after all, many similarities in the development paths followed by the East Asian countries of South Korea, Taiwan and Japan on the one hand and China on the other (but see also below).[4]

A renewed role for appropriate technology?

Kaplinsky envisages a new and increased role for appropriate technology in the changed world innovation order, based on the theory of induced innovation, as described above. But while there is obviously some truth in his argument, it is advanced somewhat uncritically and hence tends to exaggerate its impact. The point

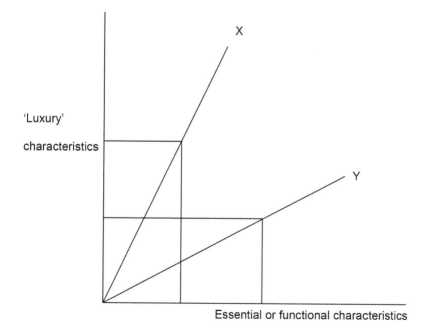

Figure 8.1 The balance of characteristics.

I wish to emphasise is that there are a number of (sometimes implicit) conditions that need to be met for the induced innovation hypothesis to work as predicted, as I will now seek to demonstrate.

On the supply side, Kaplinksy relies heavily on the rapid recent growth of R&D in China and India because it is this that largely enables private firms to make the necessary innovations in appropriate technology. There are, however, several different mechanisms that run from R&D to the predicted technology, not all of them totally convincing. For example, while such investment does often increase the technical capabilities of large local and foreign firms, it is not easy to see how this would apply to smaller firms which undertake relatively little R&D. The problem is that it is the enterprises that are typically least likely to be attracted by low-income consumers (since these firms tend to make branded goods, which rely relatively heavily on advertising and marketing).

The increased R&D, moreover, may be undertaken by multinational corporations, which export the results back to their own countries. According to Jin (2010), 'foreign companies accounted for 21 per cent (2006) of all R&D centers in large and mid-sized manufacturing .... foreign companies increased their share of total R&D expenditure in large and mid-sized manufacturing from 19.7 per cent in 2002 to 27.2 per cent in 2008, and hold 29 per cent of all invention patents in China'. This pattern, one should emphasise, differs quite markedly from the East Asian newly industrialising countries which adopted a much less enthusiastic stance towards the entry of multinationals than did China. Or again, a survey of these firms engaging in R&D in India by Prasada Reddy shows that they were generally exporting the results back to their home countries (Reddy, 1997). In this way foreign investment is diverted towards developed rather than host country needs and thus breaks the crucial link between supply and demand that is posited by induced innovation (where, in Kaplinsky's version, demand excludes the absolute poor).

Also required by the theory is the assumption that firms minimise costs, an assumption which certainly cannot be taken for granted. For, not only have plausible alternative goals been postulated (e.g., Simon's 'satisficing' or 'engineering man'),[5] but also the degree of competition may be inadequate to foster such behaviour. For example, parts of Indian industry are dominated by only a few firms, or in some cases by near monopolies (e.g., where there are pronounced economies of scale). In this respect I am inclined to think that China is generally more competitive in industry, but I have no hard evidence to support the claim. In any case, such forces of imperfect competition that undoubtedly exist in these two countries will dampen in varying degrees the operation of the induced innovation mechanism.

Still another supply-side requirement of this mechanism is that factor prices reflect their true scarcity in the economy (as opposed to the frequent price distortions in developing countries).[6] Oddly, given its importance, this issue has received scant attention in the literature. One group of authors, however, has observed that 'Underpricing of capital is probably the most important form of factor price distortion in China today' (Barclay's Capital, 2011). This phenomenon also has the effect of dampening the incentive to generate innovations that are appropriate for the poor and encourages instead the 'rapid development of capital-intensive industries'. Further aggravating the problem is the tendency towards undervaluation of the Chinese currency, which 'is a form of underpriced capital'. It is debatable whether there are also significant wage distortions in either China or India, though both countries impose minimum-wage laws (at least in the formal sector).[7]

Turning now to the demand side of the equation, much depends on whether the new good embodies a relatively heavy proportion of functional characteristics (as in the case of Nirma) or whether instead it relies heavily on marketing and advertising. A major problem for the induced innovation model in this regard is that firms tend to prefer the branded product because it increases their profits (as has been suggested, for example, in the Indian pharmaceutical industry).[8] A similar problem besets the argument made by Prahalad (2004) and others that there is a 'fortune' to be gained by selling high-quality products in small units to the billions at the bottom of the pyramid. The insistence of this point of view on high quality, however, excludes the possibility for the poor to buy less well-performing alternatives at a lower cost. In this way the size of the low-income market is reduced. Such a market, moreover,

> is unlikely to be very profitable, especially for a large company. The costs of serving the markets at the bottom of the pyramid can be very high. The poor are often geographically dispersed …. and culturally heterogeneous. This dispersion of the rural poor increases distribution and marketing costs and makes it difficult to exploit economies of scale. Weak infrastructure (transportation, communication, media, and legal) further increases the cost of doing business. Another factor leading to high costs is the small size of each transaction.
> (Karnani, 2007: 91–92)

Partly for these reasons, no more than a few studies suggest that the bottom-of-the-pyramid argument actually works in practice, especially in the case of multinationals, to whom the Prahalad argument is mainly directed (even studies dedicated to the task of finding support for the hypothesis have not turned up much).[9]

Note at this point that whereas the income group that interests Kaplinsky (between $ 1,000 and $ 5,000 p.a.) makes for more of a market for appropriate technology, it is also more attractive to users of *inappropriate* technology, that is, where relatively capital-intensive factor proportions go together with a heavily branded and highly marketed product. It is not at all clear that the former type of technology will dominate in this situation. After all, it has long been noted that the relatively poor in developing countries have a strong propensity to consume developed country–type goods, partly for the status that these goods confer (van Kempen, 2005).

Much depends, finally, on the income distribution of a country. Following Amsden (1977),

> Assume 100 economic units in market A each with an income of $ 10,000. Assume 1,000 economic units in market B each with an income of $ 1,000. Although purchasing power in the two markets is equal, obviously a market of

type A is a better candidate than a market of type B for the absorption of non-essential goods with high unit costs.

(Amsden, 1977: 218)

Market B, on the other hand, is better suited to goods which are appropriate in the sense described above. It is perhaps significant in this respect that the historically most successful examples of appropriate technology occurred in the East Asian newly industrialising countries where distribution was, at the time, notably equal (James, 1987).[10] In Indian manufacturing, by contrast, the capital-labour ratio went up quite sharply (in pharmaceuticals, for example).[11]

Appropriate technology, poverty and inequality

I have already noted that Kaplinsky assumes away the groups in absolute poverty in China, India and presumably elsewhere in the developing world.[12] I have also observed that while this assumption favours the demand side of the induced innovation mechanism, it diminishes the sense in which technology (for the non-poor) can be described as appropriate. And if poverty in the usual sense is thus excluded, so too is income distribution, the second aspect of demand in which the appropriate technology debate is traditionally grounded.[13]

What is at stake here is the comparative income level of the group or groups that benefit from a new good. These distributional effects can be substantial, since, even if a group with a relatively low income benefits from such a product, groups with higher incomes may benefit even more, causing a rise in the degree of inequality. The rapid increase in the middle class in China and India suggests that this group may well benefit most from the new branded goods designed for the local market in these countries (consider in this regard the ultra low-cost car designed by a large-scale Indian firm for the domestic market).[14]

Conceptually, the role played by new products in the distribution of welfare can be shown by using a diagram based on Lancaster's theory of demand, in which, as noted above, goods are thought of as bundles of characteristics – rays from the origin – and the distance along each ray is dependent on the consumer's income, as shown in Figure 8.2.

Assume that characteristic 1 denotes low-income characteristics and characteristic 2 represents high-income. The new product Z thus reflects more of the latter-type characteristics:

> Where the new product leaves existing products unaffected, no group of consumers will lose, but the gains from the new product will be concentrated among high-income consumers. Suppose high-income consumers have indifference map II.... With the introduction of new product Z, they will move from $I^{\circ}I^{\circ}$ to the higher indifference curve $I'I$.
>
> (James and Stewart, 1981)

In general, relative gains will be concentrated among consumers whose preferences are in favour of the characteristic that is most reduced in cost.

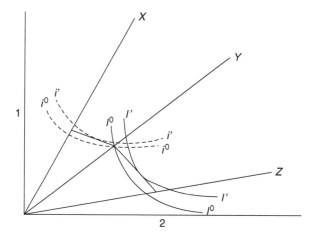

Figure 8.2 The effect of a new good on the distribution of welfare.
Source: Courtesy of James and Stewart, 1981.

Conclusions

In a recent article Kaplinksy has drawn attention to some important aspects of the new global innovation system. He has argued primarily that appropriate technology will function quite differently in this order compared to the situation in the 1970s. Indeed, it is said to have undergone nothing less than a sea change in the process, becoming closely served by private firms as opposed to NGOs.

I have argued by contrast that the author overestimates the change in the role of appropriate technology over the said period. On the one hand, he underestimates the extent to which this type of technology was used by private enterprises in certain East Asian countries in the earlier period; and, on the other hand, overestimates the extent to which the model of induced innovation will give rise to a wide spread of appropriate technology in the current situation in China and India. (He helps his case considerably in this respect by excluding the absolute poor and focusing instead on the group beyond the poverty line but less than the income of the middle class. This comes at the cost, though, of a markedly diminished sense in which technology can be described as appropriate.)

Induced innovation, I suggested, requires a number of more or less stringent conditions to be met before it works in the way that is assumed. There is very little evidence, however, on what is now occurring – it is indeed taking place 'under the radar'. If this is to change, cases dedicated to the triangular relationships between technological change, product characteristics and income will need to be undertaken across different sectors in China and India, along the lines perhaps of James (1977) and Baron and van Ginneken (1984). Essential to these cases will be a consumer expenditure survey that captures the spending on alternative products in a given market by different income groups.

Notes

1 See below the description of the Nirma case in India.
2 Ranis and Saxonhouse (1983) point to the lack of incentives to innovate in India. More specifically, commissions were not linked to profits.
3 On the ease of substituting labour for capital in different industries see Forsyth et al. (1982).
4 On the similarities see Boltho and Weber (2009).
5 Engineering man is concerned with getting the most recent technology regardless of the implications for costs.
6 On factor price distortions in developing countries, see Todaro and Smith (2011).
7 Average monthly wages in manufacturing in China are $ 110.80 as compared with $ 23.80 in India.
8 See www.springer.com/odo//content
9 See Karnani (2007).
10 In China, by contrast, the income distribution is notably unequal.
11 See endnote number 8.
12 Kaplinsky defends the exclusion of the absolute poor on the shaky grounds that this group has no disposable income. In so doing he follows an old and somewhat outdated tradition in development studies. That tradition ignores the fact that some highly divisible products in areas such as soft drinks, mobile phones and detergents can be made available even to the poorest groups. In China, for example,

> Coke came up with a drink that combines the ingredients of plain old orange juice .... with calcium, vitamins and lots of water. The diluted drink costs about $ 0.30 for a 500 ml. container. .... The results have been staggering, particularly in poor regions, where the usual orange drink sold by Coca-Cola's Minute Maid subsidiary would be unaffordable.
>
> (*The Economist*, 2007)

Whether absolute poor groups actually benefit from this product is an open question, but, along with products such as mobile phones, it interrogates the assumption that the poor have *no* disposable income.

The problem with that assumption is that the absolute poor are known on occasion to 'make room' for non-basic products. According to anthropologists such as Douglas and Isherwood (1979), the disdain accorded by economists to conspicuous consumption by the poor is unwarranted. It is based on the erroneous idea that 'physical needs are more important than psychological ones' (van Kempen, 2005). The need for status by the poor is in fact a pervasive one in the anthropological literature on consumer demand. See Douglas & Isherwood (1979) for a clear statement of this point of view.

13 See James and Stewart (1981).
14 This is the Nano made by Tata Motors. Its experience has been recently described in *Business Week*, April 11, 2013.

Part III

Building technological capabilities

9 Trait-making for labour-intensive technology in Africa: insights from infrastructure

Introduction

As noted in Chapter 5, on the basis of data collected for nine manufacturing industries and using prices that are thought to be typical of most sub-Saharan countries, Pack (1982) has shown that relatively labour-intensive techniques generate not only substantially more employment than capital-intensive alternatives, but more value-added as well. There is also evidence, however, from case studies of the region that governments exhibit a strong preference for the latter over the former techniques in those same sectors.[1]

When they are combined, these findings are often taken to imply that substantial gains in output, employment and equality, can readily accrue to governments prepared to make the implicitly costless switch from existing to labour-intensive methods of production.

As I see it, however, this conclusion rests on an (implicit) underestimation of the extent to which the labour-intensive alternatives demand change of one kind or another in the existing environment (such alternatives, that is to say, demand the 'making' of certain project traits, as opposed to the opposite form of behaviour, which implies a decision to accept some traits of a technology or project as 'temporarily unchangeable aspects of the environment').[2] The first part of the chapter sets out to describe not only the origin of this important feature of the literature, but also the specific types of traits that are neglected thereby. Thereafter and again with the help of certain Hirschmanian concepts, I employ case-study evidence to suggest how these neglected traits can best be provided in support of a wider application of labour-intensive techniques in sub-Saharan Africa. This is a policy issue, we should emphasise, which has by no means disappeared as a result of structural adjustment and other reforms in the region. For, according to a report from the World Bank (1995), 'although potential gains from privatization and other reforms are substantial, only a few countries have reformed their state-owned enterprises successfully' (1995:2). Indeed, 'In most developing countries, particularly the poorest, bureaucrats run as large a share of the economy as ever' (1995:1). Ten years later, in 2005, Nellis wrote that 'a good percentage of industrial/manufacturing and most infrastructure still remains in state hands' (Nellis, 2005).

The underestimation of trait-making for labour-intensive techniques

More than 30 years ago, in his extensive study of a diverse range of development projects, Hirschman (1967) pointed to a general tendency for planners in the public sector to underestimate the amount of trait-making that would be necessary for a successful outcome of the projects they administered. At one point, for example, he refers to 'situations in which the project planners were unaware to what extent the good fortune of their project was implicitly premised on trait-making, that is, on making over the social, economic, and human reality of their country in one way or another' (Hirschman, 1967:140). At another point, what he described as a 'persistent failure' to observe 'the very real links between sociopolitical structure and project behavior' suggested to him a 'serious and systematic neglect of an area that can be crucial to the performance of the project' (1967:145). The general point, as he saw it, is that 'development projects are likely to imply far more would-be trait-making than is commonly realized.... Bringing as they do, new activities into a pre-existing environment' (1967:145). What Hirschman concluded from observations such as these was that 'project planners ought to become sensitive to situations in which the amount of trait-making required for the success of a project is substantial, particularly when the contemplated project *must compete against another activity that is not nearly as demanding*' (1967:140, emphasis added).

In the area of technology choice, unfortunately, Hirschman's advice has, with few exceptions gone largely unheeded, especially, but not only in the context of Africa. For, as I see it, there has been a distinct tendency for the literature in this area to underestimate the amount of trait-making that is needed for the application of labour- as opposed to capital-intensive techniques, a tendency that has made it difficult to understand, and hence to correct, the fact that policymakers commonly choose the latter techniques over the former. Since many of these neglected traits are of an institutional nature, one can argue that in comparison with the very large literature on appropriate (labour-intensive) *technology*, remarkably little has been written about the appropriate *institutions* that such technologies often demand (and more specifically about the institutional innovations that will be required if labour-intensive technologies are to be introduced not merely at the small, decentralised level, but also on a large, macro-economic basis).

Much of the problem, it seems, originates in the traditional conceptualisation of the choice of techniques in a two-factor world, where the only dimensions are capital and labour. This depiction of the issue is unrealistic, among other reasons, because of the implications of the fact that the real choice is often not between one plant using capital-intensive methods and another plant using a higher ratio of labour to capital. In most cases, it is, rather, between a single, large-scale plant using capital-intensive methods and a larger (in some cases, much larger) number of labour-intensive units of production. For, as shown in Table 9.1 across a selected sample of African manufacturing industries, a single capital-intensive plant often requires far more labour-intensive units to produce the same level of output. This, in turn, means that further dimensions will enter into the choice of technique, apart from just the two traditional factors, capital and labour. In particular, not only will more entrepreneurs be required to run the additional labour-intensive units of production, but also those additional units will themselves impose organisational demands in the public sector.[3] The road construction industry provides an indication of the additional supervisory capabilities that are associated with labour, as compared to capital-based methods. According to Stock and de Veen (1996:14), for example, 'A bulldozer can be operated by one or two skilled workers, but more than a dozen supervisors are needed to oversee labourers doing the equivalent amount of work. In addition, labour is often deployed over a wider geographical area, requiring a dispersal of supervision, which further raises supervision requirements'. The problem is that in much of Africa both entrepreneurs and organisational capabilities in the public sector are in particularly short supply.[4] In relation to one country in that region, Tanzania, for example, what Clark (1978) argued many years ago is still substantially true, namely, that 'capital is not the most scarce resource. Rather, both entrepreneurs, people with ability to initiate projects, and managers, people with the ability to operate them, are in short supply' (1978:212).

Once the need for making these traits is recognised, moreover, further policy issues arise, and these too have received relatively scant attention in the literature on the choice of technology. The uncertainty that will attend most attempts to make the entrepreneurial and organisational traits needed by labour-intensive technologies, for example, will usually be unappealing to policymakers under pressure to produce quick results, especially in comparison to large-scale, capital-intensive turnkey projects, which can be carried out more swiftly and with the greater degree of certainty that comes with the ability to simply import the missing traits with foreign finance (especially, but not only, foreign aid). The danger, here, as with all attempts at trait-making in development projects, is, as Hirschman (1967) himself pointed out, 'that the desirable traits which are required for an adequate functioning of the project will simply *not* be "made" – that is, learned in time – with dire results for the project's success' (1967:135).[5] Trait-making for labour-intensive techniques on a large scale is made all the more dangerous, moreover, by the fact that institutional change of a rather fundamental type may often be required in the context of

Table 9.1 Number of labour-intensive plants to produce output equivalent of one capital-intensive plant, selected African countries and sectors

Sector (country)	Number of plants
Bricks (Botswana)	
Capital-intensive	1
Labour-intensive	11
Bread (Tanzania)	
Automated	1
Labour-intensive	50

(continued)

Table 9.1 Continued

Sector (country)	Number of plants
Sugar (Kenya)	
Vacuum-pan method	1.3
Open-pan method	
100 tons	81
200 tons	41
Maize milling (Tanzania)	
Maize roller (120 tpd)	1
Maize hammer (4 tpd)	30
Footwear (Tanzania)	
Large-scale	1
Small-scale	142

Sources: Respectively, Kaplinsky, 1990; Green, 1978; Kaplinsky, 1987; Bagachwa, 1992; Roemer et al., 1976.

Africa (in connection, for example, with the relationships between labour-intensive technology and the degree of state centralisation, or the ways in which the uncertainties and risks associated with such technology may be reduced by appropriate institutions of one kind or another).

Below, we shall consider how these difficulties can be overcome in order to promote the wider application of labour-intensive technologies in sub-Saharan Africa. Much of the case-study literature that will be used for this purpose is drawn from experience with the road-construction industry. This, we should note, is less a matter of coincidence than it is a reflection of the fact that some of the most successful cases in the region have taken place with regard to the construction, repair and maintenance of various types of roads. There are also some examples from industry, though they, also, are somewhat dated. The problem is that, as noted throughout the earlier chapters, there are very few choice of technique studies in Africa over the past 20 years or so. I am confident, however, that the issues raised by the examples given in this chapter are still relevant today.

Trait-making for labour-intensive technology

Risk and uncertainty

As already noted, trait-making in general is prone to the risk that the missing traits on which the success of a project crucially depends, will not in fact be supplied. 'Under what conditions' then, asks Hirschman (1967), 'is the risk sufficiently small that trait-making becomes a practical possibility?' 'The most obvious answer', he believed,

> is that many traits, from simple skills to administrative ability, can be slowly learned 'on the job' or alongside it. The fact that these traits are not yet available in the desired quantity and quality at the inception of the project can mean simply that the cost of construction and operation of the project should make allowance for the inevitable learning process to which outside education and training will of course be expected to make an important contribution. It is precisely because much trait-making proceeds through gradual 'on the job' learning that latitude for poor performance can be a welcome attribute of projects.
>
> (Hirschman, 1967:153)

Hirschmanian latitudes

By the term 'latitude', Hirschman (1967) refers to those characteristics of a project that permit 'The project planner and operator to mold it, or let it slip, in one direction or another, regardless of outside occurrences' (1967:86). Latitude in a project may derive from at least two sources: one having to do with time and the other with the nature of the characteristics embodied in the ultimate output of the project. 'Temporal latitudes' imply that at each of the various stages through which a project progresses, allowances can be made with respect to the amount of time required for the necessary traits to be made (as opposed to the lack of latitude that inheres in the so-called time-bound project). Product quality latitudes recognise that standards appropriate to one context may not be appropriate to another. Moreover, these latitudes recognise that labour-intensive techniques are often incapable, from an engineering point of view, of producing exactly the same product characteristics as capital-intensive alternatives (among other reasons, because of the closer tolerances that the latter is usually able to achieve).

Both temporal and quality latitudes played an important role in what is still arguably the most extensive application of labour-intensive techniques in sub-Saharan Africa, namely, the Rural Access Roads Programme (RARP) in Kenya, which has constructed thousands of kilometres of access and minor roads, on the basis of labour-based methods. Let us consider first the temporal latitudes that were allotted to this programme in the name of trait-making (that is to say, on the basis of an explicitly recognised need to develop the various indigenous capabilities associated with the application of labour-intensive technology on so unprecedented a scale). To quote Edmonds and Ruud (1984),

> The programme had a very slow build up…. Thus in the first 3 years output was low. This was a result of a *quite deliberate policy decision*. It was recognized that this was a totally new programme for Kenya using a technology which was not widely understood. Time was, therefore, required to modify and adapt the existing procedures and to develop a suitable training programme.
>
> (Edmonds and Ruud, 1984:15)

During this trait-making intensive phase (that lasted from 1975 to 1980), RARP enjoyed the considerable expatriate support that Hirschman envisaged (in the quotation from him that was provided at the beginning of this section). By 1980, however, after extensive trait-making had indeed taken place among the local labour force at various levels, the foreign presence, according to Edmonds and Ruud (1984), was 'drastically reduced both in quantity and orientation' (1984:16).[6] I turn now to examine Hirschman's quality latitudes.

Similarly, in Botswana, where another successful large-scale, labour-based road construction programme subsequently took place,

> Between 1980 and 1989, 145 people (55 of them women) were trained as road builders, in addition 11 people were trained as multi-site supervisors and six as district level co-ordinators. Whereas by the end of 1983 only some 200 km of road had been improved and less than 200 people employed at any one time, by 1990 over 2000 km had been upgraded and over 3000 people employed (per year). *It can be seen that as for Kenya the lead-in time is extensive, partly because of the fact that one is establishing and staffing an institution.*
>
> (McCutcheon, 1995:341, emphasis added)

Table 9.2 Quality latitudes in road construction

Dimension of choice	*Quality latitudes for labour-based methods*
Project design	'Designs that support the use of labour-based methods minimize the moving of earth in a longitudinal direction. Designers can reduce earthmoving by following the contours of the terrain where it is feasible (for example, in rural areas with little traffic), by locating smaller borrow pits at more frequent intervals and by achieving earthworks by cross movements rather than by extensive longitudinal movements' (1996:17).
Type of materials	'The type of materials selected for a project often dictates the technology that must be used. For example, choosing graded crushed stone for the base courses in black-top surfaced roads automatically dictates the use of equipment based methods … choosing concrete and reinforced concrete structures may dictate the use of more equipment-based methods than choosing local materials, such as treated hard wood, masonry or brick, which may be acceptable alternatives' (1996:17).
Design standards	'In order not to bias designs against labour-based methods, design engineers must specify acceptable (not maximum) standards. For example, designing structures with lower concrete strengths and increased dimensions would allow the use of hand-broken, lower-strength aggregates. Compaction standards should also be specified with care, since these standards can also dictate the choice of technology, particularly on unsurfaced (gravel or earth) roads. Often design engineers stipulate – unjustifiably – that the high compaction standards necessary for paved roads, also be met for unpaved roads' (1996:17).

Source: Stock and de Veen, 1996.

Apparently, the gradual learning that Hirschman envisaged when a degree of latitude is present in a project can be achieved in Africa under the appropriate circumstances.

In Kenya, RARP also exploited certain quality latitudes that favour the use of labour- over capital-intensive methods of production. As shown in Table 9.2, these types of latitudes fall into three categories, namely, those having to do with project design, the choice of materials and design standards. (The examples cited in that table are meant to be illustrative rather than an exhaustive description of all the available latitudes.)

The Kenyans made particular use of the quality latitudes that are available in constructing and maintaining access and minor, as opposed to main, roads. Being subject to less intensive use, for example, the former allow a greater degree of latitude in horizontal and geometric design standards than the latter. Access and minor roads, moreover, can be built with less precision than major roads, and to this extent there is more scope for labour-based methods. With regard to the 'compaction of earthworks and the final surfacing', for example, 'it is true that it is extremely difficult to provide the same standard using labour-based methods' (Edmonds & Howe, 1980:18).

In many other sectors in Kenya, as elsewhere in Africa, however, the scope for quality latitudes – and hence for the use of labour-based techniques – has been unnecessarily restricted by the use of developed country inputs and design latitudes. Thus,

> Standards, and specifications for building materials production and use, for example are one of the most indispensable features of regulations and codes. In the absence of appropriate standards and specifications for building materials … most building regulations and codes (in Africa) make reference to foreign standards. Hence, an adverse impact on the promotion of locally produced and low-cost building materials. This frequent reference to foreign standards has also led to the use of building materials and construction techniques with high import content.
>
> (Der-Petrossian, 1995:7)

In its turn,

> the presence of high cost and import-based building materials and construction techniques which dominate the provisions of existing regulations and codes has had a negative influence on construction practices for the low-income population. In some instances, simple rural dwellings have been constructed in reinforced concrete technology at prohibitive costs.
>
> (Der-Petrossian, 1995:8)

Conversely, the adoption of lower, or intermediate, standards for building materials would not only make housing and shelter more available to the low-income majority in Africa, but also it would enable the wider use of labour-based methods of construction.[7]

This conclusion is also of particular importance to the small-scale sector of African manufacturing, which, I have suggested, should play a greater role in an employment-intensive industrialisation strategy. For, this sector typically makes widespread use of quality latitudes when producing for local or regional markets, where demands for quality are less stringent than they are for average- and high-income buyers in developed countries. In the latter types of markets, there may be few or no alternatives to a trait-taking, foreign-dominated type approach, though there might still be a demand for labour-intensive products among those with relatively low incomes, whose preferences are based on price rather than brand or marketing appeal.

Trait-taking is also more likely when planners are in hurry to show results. Thus, according to Wangwe (1992:239),

> The desire to implement projects with as little delay as possible tended to overshadow any concerns with technological learning. Concerns with speed of project implementation were overriding; the use of foreign finance packaged with foreign personnel was deemed the most appropriate for the attainment of this objective.

Yet another reason for taking traits is an unfavourable attitude held by policymakers towards the production factor whose characteristics need to be 'made'. For example, in explaining the failure of certain road construction projects in Africa, McCutcheon (2008) refers to a view that

> one of the major stumbling blocks is the perception that labour-intensive work is simple work by simple people in simple places using simple tools and, therefore, there is no need for sophisticated people to take the matter seriously – consequently no need to plan. No appreciation of the need for development skills.
>
> (McCutcheon, 2008:27)

Pilot projects

We have already described how Hirschmanian latitudes can be used to lessen the risk and uncertainty associated with trait-making for labour-based methods of production in sub-Saharan Africa. We turn now to an additional tool that can be employed for this same purpose, namely, the pilot project. It is useful to distinguish between at least two forms that such projects can take, because they serve different purposes and contain different mechanisms through which the reduction of risk and uncertainty is effected.[8] On the one hand, that is to say, pilot projects can be used to test, on an experimental basis, whether the new approach is likely to be successful on a larger scale. On the other hand, pilot projects can also be used to demonstrate (on a small scale) that a new approach is actually feasible. (The distinction is hence between the testing and promotion of new projects on a small scale.)

In the road construction sector in Africa, pilot projects appear to have taken mainly the latter form, and, as noted by Stock and de Veen (1996), they have often succeeded in this demonstrative role:

> Pilot projects can help promote acceptance. In general, governments in the developing world doubt the efficiency of labour-based methods, preferring

to pass the risk of their initial implementation to aid agencies. Experiences in Chad, Ghana, … Kenya and Mozambique prove that once labour-based schemes are shown to produce high quality roads in a cost-effective manner, they become politically attractive to the host government, which thereafter provides counterpart support.

(Stock and de Veen, 1996:14)

Conceived as such, moreover, pilot projects in one country can help to convince policymakers in other, similar countries. Here again it is worth referring to the Kenya RARP and in particular to the 'study tour' of the programme that was provided to engineers and economists from other African countries, under the auspices of the International Labour Office and the Kenyan Ministry of Works. The participants were invited to visit some of the field activities and to discuss the programme with the officials most closely involved with it (de Veen, 1980). Subsequently, and based partly on that experience, a number of African countries (such as Botswana and Ethiopia) themselves embarked on pilot road construction projects based on labour-intensive methods (Edmonds and Ruud, 1984). In general, it appears that 'study tours have been particularly effective at changing attitudes in the Africa region' (Stock and de Veen, 1996:14).

Unfortunately, however, the pilot project approach has not always been used as a means of demonstrating the viability of labour-intensive alternatives to large-scale, capital-intensive methods of production in Africa. According to Green (1978), for example, part of an alternative to the controversial choice of a large-scale automated bakery in Tanzania (to which we alluded above) would have been to 'identify and support a group (or groups) interested in creating one to three test cooperative, small-scale, hand bakeries and to experiment with ways of providing procurement and marketing services to the hand bakery' (1978:19). No such experiments were forthcoming, however.

Decentralisation

Decentralisation within the public sector

Though they are not often identified in the literature, there are several reasons why the delegation of authority to local government facilities may even be demanded by use of labour-based methods. One such reason has something to do with the relationship between decentralisation and project design, and in particular the fact that

Decentralization places decision-making where heavy equipment is often less readily available, where engineers who favour equipment-based techniques are not concentrated, and where equipment-based contractors do not see big stakes … Thus, local government entities are likely to espouse a simpler technology that favours the use of labour rather than equipment.

(Stock and de Veen, 1996:23)

A second reason has to do more with the political economy of technical choice, and although the following citation refers to the case of road works, it also applies more generally. For what is essentially at issue is:

> enlarging and strengthening the domestic constituency in favour of labour-based methods. In centralized programs, often the only stakeholders supporting labour-based methods other than the donors financing the program are the small farmers in rural areas who work on the road sites, and the small-scale contractors who have little access to equipment. In decentralized programs, however, the set of stakeholders grows to include local civil servants. These civil servants support labour-based methods because of their simplicity – they enable civil servants to manage road works that would have been managed at a higher level if carried out with equipment-based methods. In addition, decentralization often makes it easier for the supporters of labour-based methods (the contractors, the local officials, and the small farmers who work as labourers) to press their demands on government, since they may have more power at the local level and are closer to where management decisions are made.
>
> (Stock and de Veen, 1996:24)

From both these points of view, it is unfortunate that in most African countries the state is run along highly centralised lines. In fact, for reasons that have to do both with internal political factors as well as a tendency for foreign aid donors to bypass 'secondary structures in favour of relationships with central authorities' (Picard, 1994:8),[9] the African state is highly centralised even by Third World standards.[10]

That so extreme a degree of state centralisation might hinder even the espoused political goal of promoting labour-intensive methods was recognised many years ago, as the following quotation from Phillips (1979), in the context of early Tanzanian industrialisation, well illustrates.[11] In particular, he argued that:

> the pattern of investment input and output is determined by the 'locus' of control over the means of production. Technology will similarly be dependent on this control structure, and the degree to which small-scale labour-intensive techniques are possible depends on the degree of decentralization of control and ownership. The Tanzanian economy is characterised by centralised control, strongly influenced by external trade and foreign technology and capital dependence. It follows that Tanzania's objective of relocation of industry and small-scale industrial development will not be achieved, *and technological alternatives will not be adopted, unless a far-reaching redistribution of control occurs in industry*, involving local enterprises, cooperatives, district development corporations and other organizations able to control appropriation and distribution of investable surpluses, bank credit, savings, employment policy, raw material supplies and markets.
>
> (Phillips, 1979:86, emphasis added)

It was also not long after the Arusha Declaration of 1967 that precisely this problem emerged in the choice of technology for the bakery project in Tanzania, to which we have already referred in a number of other contexts. On the one hand, in addition to the traits that needed to be made in those other contexts, the hand-baking alternative also ran into a major organisational problem, namely, that 'there was no evident decentralised public sector institution to operate (them)' (Green, 1978:15). The large-scale, automated bakery, on the other hand, fitted very readily into the centralised state apparatus, through which foreign finance was generally administered without much regard to the technological aspects of development projects.[12]

It is, of course, true that since then in Africa, as indeed most other parts of the Third World, attempts have been made to strengthen local governments. Indeed, according to one observer (Manor, 1995), 'Decentralization has quietly become one of the fashions of our time' (1995:81). And in some African countries there has been undeniable progress towards meeting this objective.[13] Yet, overall reviews of the African experience tend to suggest that progress towards a more decentralised state has at best been rather limited. Garrity and Picard (1994), for example, represent the then predominant view among authorities on the subject when they conclude that

> Throughout Africa, policy elites have been less than successful in decentralizing policy-making and administration.... Both decentralization and pluralism have foundered on lack of resources (physical and human) a lack of skills, and the lack of political will to commit to devolved, participatory government.
>
> (1994:156)

There is, however, at least one example from the region which attests to the positive influence that decentralisation can exert in favour of labour-based methods, on those (relatively rare) occasions when it has been successfully implemented. I am referring here to the case of the non-gazetted road network in Botswana, as reported by McCutcheon (1995). In particular,

> Under its policies of decentralization and rural development, responsibility for non-gazetted roads had been given to the District Councils which were autonomous bodies falling under the overall jurisdiction of the Ministry of Local Government and Lands (MLGL). In 1980, a pilot project of labour-intensive "district road" construction and maintenance was initiated in the Central District.... Eventually, a successful programme was established and many key aspects are similar to the RARP (the Kenyan Rural Access Roads Programme).
>
> (1995:341)

Engineers working on the gazetted road network in Botswana, by contrast, had steadfastly 'refused to countenance the use of labour-intensive methods'. One should add here the observation by McCutcheon and Parkins (2009:206) that,

Unless the consultants have been thoroughly trained, they cannot design labour-intensive projects, or prepare appropriate contract documentation, … The same applies to the need for contractors and site-supervisors to be properly trained. Added to these factors is the prevailing prejudice in the civil construction industry against labour-intensive construction.

Decentralisation outside the public sector

As opposed to decentralisation that takes place within the public sector itself, decentralisation to non-state actors occurs when governments permit privately owned firms and voluntary organisations to perform tasks formerly undertaken by enterprises owned by the state. As part of structural adjustment reforms and privatisation programmes, this latter form of decentralisation became increasingly relevant during and after that period.

Compared, for example, to the period of African socialism in Tanzania when the choice of the automated bakery was made, the scope for decentralisation to small-scale, privately owned firms and voluntary organisations in that country has widened considerably, as the experience in the oil-processing sector well illustrates. In particular, on the basis of a low-cost, labour-intensive technology known as the RAM press, and with assistance provided, among other institutions, by what was then Appropriate Technology International (an American-based NGO), no fewer than 2,000 new enterprises have been created in Tanzania and Zimbabwe, with the benefits accruing mainly to those located in dispersed/rural areas. It appears thus that the project has been highly successful not only in making scarce entrepreneurial traits but also the capabilities needed to operate the small-scale technology. As in the case of RARP in Kenya, however, the making of the traits that are required for applying labour-intensive technology on so large a scale was not achieved in a matter of months. Rather, 'the Tanzanian (oil processing) experience indicated the importance of a sustained, gradual approach to technology transfer with a time horizon of five years or more' (Hyman, 1993:442).

What also needs to be emphasised is that this form of decentralisation (to actors outside the public sector) is complementary to, rather than independent of, decentralisation within the public sector itself. The reason is that highly centralised systems of government tend to be ill-informed about and hence tend to underestimate the potential afforded by small-scale, labour-intensive firms in the private sector.

An example of how capacities of local firms are often underestimated by central government ministries is provided by Burundi and Tanzania, where private sector firms have been contracted by local governments to build sections of roads even as their respective Highway Authorities were unaware of such activities and did not know that such private contractors were available with their own road equipment.

(Silverman, 1992:12)

Conclusions

In this chapter, I have sought to revive an observation, advanced originally by Hirschman (1967), that development projects tend to require much more change in the existing socio-economic environment than is commonly supposed (in his terms, that is to say, more traits need to be 'made' than is commonly thought, in order for development projects to be successful). More specifically, what I have argued is that if labour-intensive technological choices are to be applied more widely than has hitherto occurred in Africa, far more attention needs to be paid to trait-making of an institutional kind, especially, but not only, because of the fact that in reality the choice confronting policymakers is between a single, large-scale, capital-intensive plant and a (much) larger number of small-scale, labour-intensive units of production (as opposed to the traditional depiction of this choice as being between a *single* plant which is either capital- or labour-intensive).

Some degree of institutional trait-making will need to be undertaken, for example, with respect to the risk and uncertainty that is bound to attend the introduction (on a large scale) of labour-based methods of production, many of whose features will be new to an industrial environment where large-scale, foreign-financed projects embodying few attempts at local trait-making tend to be very much the norm. In addition it is likely that the design and administration of numerous small-scale, labour-intensive units of production (often located in dispersed rural areas) will require a far more decentralised set of institutions than currently exists in most of Africa. Note here that decentralisation is itself a trait that needs to be made, not just once-and-for-all but over time as well. As Kauzya (2007:15) has put it,

> The experience of Uganda, Rwanda, and South Africa also illustrate that ... the process of agreeing the exercise of shared power and authority should not be taken for granted. Which ever approach applied, support for decentralization comes through patient and sustained negotiation, sensitization, persuasion, demonstration of positive results, and sometimes, when necessary coercion. The three cases also show that decentralization is not a one time action but an on-going process that constantly engages the relevant stakeholders and actors.

The discussion of these relatively neglected problems of institutional trait-making forms the main part of our analysis, which, again, relies partly on certain Hirschmanian concepts and which draws mainly on examples from the area of road construction and maintenance, where many of the most extensive applications of labour-based methods have occurred in Africa. What appears to be common to these successful cases is that the necessary amount of institutional trait-making was explicitly taken into account in project design and implementation, not only by the state but also by foreign aid donors or international agencies. And because the state still operates in the industrial sector in many African countries, this policy conclusion has by no means lost its relevance to contemporary technological choices in those same countries.

Though they have been applied largely to infrastructure in this chapter, Hirschman's categories also apply to parts of manufacturing in Africa, as I have demonstrated in numerous examples. As such, these categories help to explain what has long seemed paradoxical in African manufacturing, namely, that technical choices are often made in favour of capital- rather than labour-intensive methods. Such choices, I have suggested, are usually made in a three- rather than two-factor world and should be framed as such for policy analysis.

Appendix: Choice of technology in three dimensions

Figure 9A.1 depicts not only the two usual dimensions of technical choice, but also a third dimension, representing entrepreneurial/organisational capabilities. The latter, however, is associated with only one of the three capital-labour ratios I have identified in the diagram. The first two ratios, K_3L_3 and K_1L_1, represent the choice between a single large-scale, capital-intensive plant and one smaller-scale, relatively labour-intensive unit of production, respectively. It can be seen that neither of these methods makes any demands on the third factor, and it is indeed precisely the choice between these two methods that is implicit in the existing literature.

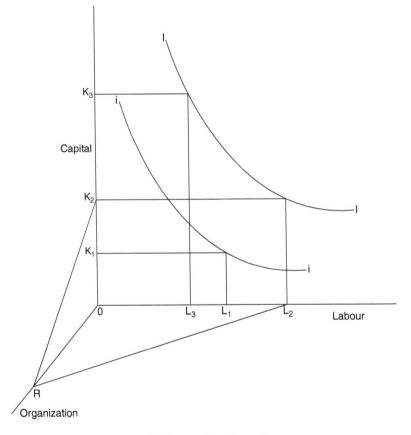

Figure 9A.1 The choice of technology in three dimensions.
Source: James, 1999.

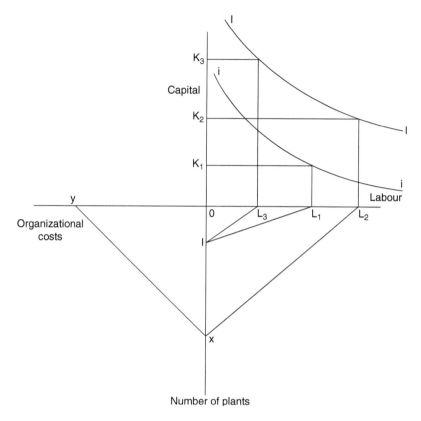

Figure 9A.2 The relationship between factor intensity and number of plants.
Source: James, 1999.

The third ratio, K_2L_2, on the other hand, does require entrepreneurial/organisational capabilities (equal to, say, OR) because it requires more than a single plant to produce the higher level of output associated with K_1L_1 (on the isoquant II rather than the isoquant ii). This distinction is shown more explicitly in Figure 9A.2, which contains three quadrants rather than three dimensions. The first quadrant contains the same information about capital-labour ratios as Figure 9A.1, but the second quadrant indicates the number of plants that is associated with each ratio. And whereas the capital-intensive and small-scale labour-intensive methods, K_1L_1 and K_3L_3, are associated (by previous assumption) with only one plant, the larger-scale labour-intensive technique, K_2L_2, requires a greater number, equal to, say, OX. The third quadrant, in turn, displays the extent of additional costs that are associated with technique K_2L_2, an amount which I have arbitrarily assumed in the figure to equal OY. These costs have to be factored in to the true choice of technique.

Notes

1　This evidence is reviewed in James (1995).
2　This distinction is due to Hirschman (1967). It also forms the core of the discussion in James (1999). The present chapter, however, although overlapping with the latter citation, is more concerned with the policy aspects of trait-making for labour-intensive techniques.
3　For a diagrammatic exposition of this point, see appendix.
4　In the aforementioned study of Pack (1982) of the gains in employment and value-added that could be reaped from switching to labour-intensive methods in Africa, this problem is dismissed by assuming 'that the supply of managers and operatives is sufficient to enable a larger number of smaller plant to be established simultaneously' (1982:6)
5　The controversial bakery case in Tanzania described by Green (1978) well seems to illustrate this problem. For, on the one hand, small-scale hand-baking technology saves on both capital and import costs relative to the automated, large-scale alternative. And since the spare parts associated with the hand-bakeries could have been locally produced, such technology would also have helped to foster the indigenous capital goods sector. Yet, the public sector institution in question nevertheless chose the automated bakery, which was financed with Canadian aid. Part of the reason for this apparently inappropriate decision was the lack of hand-baking experience 'and of successful producer cooperative experience generalizable to new ventures' (1978:18). These factors, understandably, meant that starting 40 or 50 small bakeries would have been prone to considerable risk and uncertainty. In this light, the choice that was made does not seem as irrational as it has sometimes been depicted.
6　Apart thus from the replacement of foreign by local personnel, the Kenyans also managed to create a more favourable institutional environment for labour-based methods of road construction. For example,

> The Kenyan government trains all foremen and overseers in both equipment- and labour-based methods. This policy creates greater uniformity in career paths. Career development in labour-based works can also lead to international opportunities. A number of Kenyan – engineers who became involved in the labour-based program later found employment internationally as labour-based experts. The ability to vie for international opportunities may be further incentive for staff to join a labour-based department (Stock and de Veen, 1996:15).

7　Hirschman (1967:124) himself recognised this need when discussing the inadequacy of 'standards prevailing in the developed countries' in the context of poor countries. He saw that 'A tendency to depart from the accepted standards may represent an attempt to find a more appropriate solution, rather than mere slippage' (1967:125).
8　For a fuller discussion of this point, see James (1989).
9　In Madagascar, for example, 'decisions on public investments of regional and local interest … have remained mainly determined at the central level and almost entirely externally financed by the donor community' (World Bank, 1999:2).
10　For empirical confirmation of this point, see Heller and Tait (1983).
11　Clark (1978) cites many statements from Tanzania's top political leadership in favour of labour-intensive techniques in the period after the Arusha Declaration of 1967.
12　For an extensive discussion of the relationship between aid donors and the state in sub-Saharan Africa and the implications of these relationships for the choice of technology and the acquisition of indigenous technological capabilities, see James (1995).
13　See, for example, Bratton and Rothchild (1994) and Oyugi (1994).

10 A critique of macro measures of technological capabilities in an African perspective

This chapter will be guided by recognition of two points, both of which feature prominently in institutional economics, or, as it is sometimes called, institutionalism. The first point has to do with the centrality of technology to economic growth and development, while the second concerns the inappropriateness of technological and other concepts developed in rich countries for the very different circumstances prevailing in the poorer countries. Let us deal with each of these recognitions in turn.

For two of the best-known early proponents of institutionalism, Clarence Ayres and Thorstein Veblen, the role of technology in the dynamic processes of growth and development was nothing short of overridingly important. 'Ayres,' for example, 'placed more emphasis on technology than on any other factor which contributed to economic development' (Cypher and Dietz, 2004:172). Indeed, 'For Ayres, technological progress and economic development were virtually synonymous' (Cypher and Dietz, 2004:172). Writing at the turn of the century, Veblen was no less insistent on the importance of technology and technological change in the evolutionary process of cumulative change in the economy. He

> emphasized the role of technological change, broadly defined to include both hardware and know-how. He stressed industrial arts to a point that bordered on determinism. The adage, necessity is the mother of invention, was reversed; invention had become the mother of necessity.
>
> (Clark and Juma, 1988:211)

In the more recent 'new institutional economics,' moreover, some authors continue to emphasise the dominant role of technology in creating the potential for economic growth and development. To Douglass North, for example,

> The second economic revolution which began in the second half of the nineteenth century was the systematic application of the modern scientific disciplines to technology and more broadly to the economic problems of scarcity. For those economies that could realize their potential the productivity implications have resulted in standards of well-being simply unimagined by prior generations.
>
> (North, 1993:4)

By now, a large body of empirical evidence has confirmed that economic growth does indeed depend heavily on technological change (Helpman, 2004), but this evidence also points to wide variations in growth rates across countries. The focus of this chapter on technological indices can thus be viewed as an attempt to understand why some countries are able to exploit the benefits of modern technology, while others plainly lack the ability to do so (most notably, but not exclusively, countries in sub-Saharan Africa). I will in fact be concerned with the measurement of technological capabilities, which were described in previous chapters as being essential to sustained industrial development in Africa. One of the themes is that there is a substantial disconnect between micro studies of specific capabilities in developing countries (e.g., by Lall) and macro attempts to measure those capabilities. The micro studies clearly show, for example, that the ability to adopt technologies to the local context is a crucial capability, but it is not an issue that is addressed by macro measures.

Also heavily undergirding the chapter is, as noted above, the recognition that concepts designed for the rich countries may be inappropriate to the conditions prevailing in the majority of poor countries that comprise the Third World. From our particular point of view, this problem has to do with technology concepts that are transferred, as is, from rich to poor countries. Irrespective of the specific concept at issue, however, this second recognition is usually based on a rejection of the claim to a 'monoeconomics,' an economics, that is to say, which purports to apply with equal relevance to countries at very different stages of development. Among the many development economists who reject this claim to a universally applicable form of economics, two of them warrant special mention for their well-known contributions that were published in the 1960s. In *Asian Drama* (1968), Gunnar Myrdal presented a highly detailed and convincing account of the dangers involved in applying a 'Western approach' to the development problems in South Asia. 'Economic theorists,' he argued, 'more than other social scientists have long been disposed to arrive at general propositions and then postulate them as valid for every time, place and culture' (Myrdal, 1968:6). Across a wide range of development issues, Myrdal showed how this line of thought can lead to problems of mismeasurement and policy errors in the countries belonging to South Asia. In a similar vein, an influential article written by Dudley Seers (1962) points out the implausibility of deriving general propositions from the experience of relatively few industrialised economies, which, seen from a global perspective, exhibit an exceptional range of characteristics. (The typical case, by contrast, is a poor, largely rural economy, whose characteristics are very much the rule, rather than the exception, at the global level.) Seers suggested, accordingly, that those who focus (in, say, teaching) on the relatively unusual, developed countries need constantly to stress the limitation of what is, in effect, a very special case. The case is less special nowadays as certain developing countries have joined the ranks of the developed, but the overall point remains.

Existing technological indices

Most existing measures of technology capabilities at the national level have in common that they focus on technology that is relevant to the rich rather than the poor countries, that they are concerned with ownership of rather than access to technologies, that they focus on high rather than low technology and that they exclude capabilities of small-scale firms.

That I view this information as being mostly unhelpful is a matter of values and development perspectives, but even when they are evaluated on their own terms, these indicators perform poorly in discriminating among many poor countries, whose scores on indices such as patents, high-technology exports, and Internet hosts tend to be zero or negligible. In other words, my problem is partly that the UNDP could better spend its time on indices that more closely accord with its mandate, but also that the goals of the TAI (Technology Achievements Index) are themselves not met. These goals are best expressed in the words of the UNDP itself:

> The design of the index reflects two particular concerns. *First, to focus on indicators that reflect policy concerns for all countries, regardless of the level of technological development. Second, to be useful for developing countries. To accomplish this the index must be able to discriminate between countries at the lower end of the range.*
>
> (UNDP, 2001:46; emphasis added)

In expanded form, these criticisms form the first part of the chapter, and they are advanced mainly towards one of the numerous indices now in existence: to wit, the TAI proposed by the UNDP (2001). I have chosen to focus on this particular index partly because it sits so oddly with the well-known emphasis of the UNDP on problems of human development that are disproportionately represented in rural rather than urban areas and from whom one may thus have expected some attention to be paid to the technical achievements in those same areas. This critique is followed in the second, more constructive, part of the chapter, by an attempt to modify the TAI and to identify elements of an alternative approach to measuring technical achievements on the other.

Critique of the TAI (and other similar measures of technological achievement)

Other things being equal, an index that includes developed, as well as developing, countries is preferable to a measure that is relevant to just one country grouping. The former type of index is perhaps best exemplified by the Human Development Index, which is able to rank more than 160 countries, because each of its components (such as infant mortality and life expectancy) is applicable as much to rich as to poor country groupings. Indeed, it is at least partly due to this widespread applicability that the HDI has become one of the most widely used cross-country measures in the entire field of development studies.

The situation is entirely different, however, when, in the construction of an index, a bias is introduced through the selection of indicators that are relevant to one group of countries but much less so, if at all, to another group. In the case of the TAI, my contention is that it embodies a strongly developed country bias in the choice of indicators and that this bias has a number of important implications for the measurement of technological capabilities in the Third World. The first implication is that the choice of indicators relating, for example, to the creation of technology is so rarely relevant to the majority of poor countries (where only a relatively small amount of R&D is undertaken) that they do not engage the attention of institutions in the countries whose task it is to collect statistics at the national level. This, in turn, has the effect of excluding countries from the TAI that do in fact have some capabilities in the activities in question. (As we shall see below, the exclusion of developing countries is a problem that acutely besets the TAI.) Even where the necessary data are available, moreover, they are often so low as to rob the index of its discriminatory power (most especially for countries below a certain level of per capita income). The final problem, to which I have alluded above, is that the developed country bias of the TAI translates, within given countries, into an urban bias, since it is generally the urban sector that most closely reflects the conditions prevailing in the rich countries. And this latter bias, in turn, implies that technological capabilities in areas of the economy less reflective of conditions in developed countries are ignored.

Let me begin our discussion of these issues by describing the various elements that comprise the TAI and explaining why I think many of them are subject to developed country bias (and by extension to urban bias). As a general basis for my critique, I should note, however, that the earlier debate over appropriate technology is no less important than, and indeed overlaps with, the urban / developed country bias. For, in that debate, the major theme concerns the suitability of techniques from developed countries to developing countries, where, among other differences, labour is abundant relative to capital, and the price of the former tends, accordingly, to be low in relation to the latter. The topic of this chapter is technological capabilities rather than technological choice, but the debate over the latter is a clear antecedent of the criticism that will be advanced below in relation to the former.

Table 10.1 Dimensions and indicators of the TAI (2009)

Creation of technology	i	patents granted to residents per million people
	ii	receipts of royalties and licence fees
Diffusion of recent innovations	i	Internet users per 1000 people
	ii	high technology exports as % of total manufactured exports
Diffusion of old technologies	i	electric power consumption (KWh per capita)
	ii	telephone mainlines + cellular subscribers per 1000 people
Human skills development	i	gross enrolment ratio at all levels, except pre-primary
	ii	gross enrolment ratio in science, engineering, manufacturing and construction at the tertiary level

Source: Nasir et al., 2011.

The role of developed countries' bias

The four major dimensions of the TAI and the indicators associated therewith are shown in Table 10.1.

It bears emphasising at this stage that neither the dimensions nor indicators shown in Table 10.1 differ substantially from other attempts to measure technological capabilities across a wide sample of countries.[1]

The Technology Capabilities Index (ArCo) compiled by Archibugi and Coco (2004), for example, includes the following subindexes: patents, scientific articles, Internet penetration, telephone penetration, electricity consumption, tertiary science and engineering enrolment, mean years of schooling and the literacy rate.

To an apparently large extent, therefore, the charge that the TAI is subject to a developed-country / urban bias seems applicable to the other measures as well.[2] The nature and consequences of this form of bias have been most thoroughly explored by Myrdal (1968) in his *Asian Drama*, which concludes that 'when theories and concepts designed to fit the special conditions of the Western world ... are used in the study of underdeveloped countries in South Asia, where they do not fit, the consequences are serious' (Myrdal, 1968:17). One example of this general danger arises 'from the neat division of income into two parts, consumption and saving,' which is clearly plausible 'in Western societies where the general levels of income and a stratified system of income redistribution by social security policies and other means have largely abrogated any influence on productivity' (Myrdal, 1968:19). In many developing countries, on the other hand, so neat a conceptual distinction does not, as Myrdal pointed out, apply to groups living in poverty. Essentially, the reason he gave is that for many such groups, poverty tends to be accompanied by malnutrition and a consequent inability to work productively. Because of this relationship, Myrdal further suggested that expenditure on food may often exert an influence on productivity and growth that needs to be recognised at micro and macro levels of analysis. If, however, the conceptual separation of savings and consumption continues to be made, the extent of developed-country bias might, in his view, indeed be considerable.

To what extent, then, do the defining concepts and measures of the TAI, shown in Table 10.1, reflect developed rather than developing country conditions, and, if so, what are the consequences? This question can be most easily answered, I feel, in relation to the concept of 'technology creation', which is measured in terms of patents and royalties. For it is this dimension that is almost entirely dominated by rich countries, which in 2013 held nearly 60 per cent of all global patents (to whom the majority of royalties and license fees must, accordingly, have accrued). The question that then arises has to do with the consequences of using a biased measure of technological capabilities in an index that purports to cover developing as well as developed countries (a bias that, in assuming all countries strive to meet the same goals, exactly parallels what Myrdal had in mind). Note that Africa suffers the most from this bias because virtually no patents are recorded for this region.

Technology creation

Arguably, the major consequence is that the exclusive focus on technology creation, diverts attention of resources from the far more fundamental capabilities associated with the use and assimilation by developing countries, of precisely the innovations described in the previous paragraph. The need for acquiring these assimilative technological capabilities has been clearly described by Carl Dahlman and Larry Westphal (1982:105) in the following terms:

> The exploitation of technological knowledge is central to the development process. Less-developed economies typically obtain this knowledge from more advanced ones rather than by creating it themselves. This is to be expected, given the vast pool of foreign technological knowledge available to them for exploitation. It does not follow, however, that technological effort has only a minor role to play in the process of industrial development. Such an inference would only be valid if technological effort were conceived narrowly, as the employment of resources solely for the purpose of creating new knowledge. In fact, however, *resources are also needed for the task of learning to make effective use of existing knowledge.* It is in this broader and more realistic sense that the term 'technological effort' is used … i.e. as the employment of resources not just to create technical knowledge, but also to master it.
>
> (Dahlman and Westphal, 1982:105, emphasis added)

As it is, developing countries, especially those in Africa, tend to underestimate the crucial role that needs to be played in building local capabilities to make effective use of foreign technologies. (See the discussion in Chapter 9 dealing with trait-making for appropriate technology.) If such countries take the TAI seriously, they will find no reason whatever to alter their exciting technological proclivities, since only the creation of patentable technology is capable of raising the value of this index. (It is worth noting here that no such problem arises in relation to the HDI, whose components are just as important, if not more so, to developing, as opposed to developed, countries. The HDI, that is to say, does not suffer from the type of developed country bias that afflicts the technology creation component of the TAI.) Contrary to what the UNDP seems to believe, it is simply not the case that all countries view the need to increase the number of patentable innovations as a relevant policy goal.

Diffusion of the Internet

Turning now to the second dimension of the TAI, developed-country bias can again be detected, as can the attendant danger of focusing policy attention too heavily on just spreading technology as widely as possible, within developing countries. I am referring here specifically to the use of Internet hosts per capita as a measure of the diffusion of recent innovations (where the term 'Internet users' refers essentially to the number of people in the economy that are directly linked to the worldwide Internet network). In order to identify the developed-country bias associated with this measure, one has first to recognise that the adoption and diffusion of new products and technologies are not ends in themselves. For, as Amartya Sen (1985) has persuasively argued, what matters to the individual user of commodities and technologies occurs *after* they have been purchased or supplied. What matters, in other words, is how goods and technologies are actually used. And whereas one can reasonably assume that the majority of those living in the rich industrialised countries possess the capabilities to derive much of what an Internet-connected computer has to offer, this is certainly not an assumption that can be made in much of the Third World (where in some cases, even a large increase in the number of Internet hosts is not accompanied by a corresponding increase in well-being). Indeed, the relationship between the diffusion of Internet hosts and individual welfare then becomes highly variable, even though, in the description of the TAI, no recognition of this effect can be found. Instead, a much simpler line of reasoning is evinced, namely, 'All countries must adopt innovations to benefit from the opportunities of the network age' and that 'This is measured by diffusion of the Internet' (UNDP, 2001:46).

In the most extreme case, diffusion of additional Internet hosts may have no influence at all on individual well-being. That this is not a mere theoretical possibility is most readily apparent from an extensive evaluation carried out by the Canadian International Development Research Centre, which between 2000 and 2001 sampled some 3,500 respondents from five African countries in 36 telecentres and cyber cafes (the former being essentially donor-funded community access points, offering a range of ICTs, including the Internet, mainly to those living in rural areas (Etta and Wamahia, 2003). Findings from the Mozambique case well illustrate the overall findings of the survey and, in particular, the low percentage of Internet users, even when this service was readily available to the community at large. In Mozambique, as in the other countries, moreover, '[u]sers are shown to have been disadvantaged on the basis of age, gender, education, literacy levels, and socio-economic status' (Etta, 2002). This finding, I should note, is entirely consistent with the notion that individuals living in circumstances most unlike those prevailing in the developed countries will tend to benefit least from the technologies designed in and for precisely those latter conditions (a notion that, however, runs totally counter to the central tenet of catch-up theory, namely, that the most backward countries will benefit most from the technologies already available in the developed countries).[3]

In common with the first dimension of the TAI, therefore, the diffusion of Internet hosts does not itself mark the technological achievements that really matter to most developing countries, such as the capability to adapt and use foreign technologies effectively (which, as noted below, could be captured by total factor productivity measures). And again in analogy with technology creation, there is a danger that the focus of the TAI on Internet diffusion will deflect policy attention away from those more fundamental technological capabilities.[4] In numerous developing countries, for example, indigenously designed projects have arisen which greatly multiply the benefits from a single Internet host. One of the best known of these is the Kothmale Internet Project in Sri Lanka, which uses community radio to bring the benefits of the Internet to large numbers of rural inhabitants. In particular, browsing the Internet during special radio programs involves the local community in an essential way, as the following citation clearly reveals:

> In Kothmale … [t]he daily programmers respond to queries from listeners. Presenters first select relevant, reliable websites and broadcast the program with local resource persons as studio guests (e.g. doctors for a health program) who discuss the contents of the mostly English-language sites directly in the national languages. They also describe the websites and explain how they are browsing from one web page to another. Thus, listeners not only get the information they requested, but they understand how it is made available on the web. They can respond to the program and they know that essential data will remain available in the community database if they wish to make individual use of it.
>
> (Hughes, 2003:2)

Most examples of multiplying the impact of an Internet connection, however, are to be found in India, where an impressive array of local initiatives use intermediaries, rather than diffusion of Internet hosts, to reach millions of villagers. An intermediary in this sense is someone who is familiar both with the technology and the characteristics of the community that makes use of his or her services, more often than not, in the context of a small kiosk (James, 2004). Such kiosks are widely found on the street corners of many African countries (James, 2013).

Diffusion of 'old innovations'

Based on what has already been said, one might expect 'older' innovations such as telephones to present fewer problems of developed-country bias than were described in the previous section on the diffusion of the Internet. For, as I suggested there, it was at least in part the novelty and complexity of the technology that created welfare problems for members of society lacking the necessary user capabilities (such as high literacy and language skills, computer literacy and technical competence). Telephones, on the other hand, require only the most basic user capabilities and are thus less susceptible to this particular form of developed-country bias (as is often also the case with many second-hand products and techniques imported for use in developing countries, because they are more appropriate in this sense than the most modern vintages available in the developed world). Viewed historically, the point being made is that older goods and techniques were introduced at a time when socio-economic conditions (e.g., incomes, skills, technological complexity) were closer in many ways to contemporary circumstances in the Third World. As such, these goods and techniques are less likely than contemporary vintages to bypass those most acutely in need of the benefits from technical change.

On the other hand, however, the particular indicator chosen to reflect telephone diffusion in the TAI does contain a developed- rather than a developing-country view of how this mode of communication is actually used in the society. For, whereas in developed countries, use of the telephones occurs overwhelmingly on the basis of individual ownership, in rural and informal urban parts of developing countries it is very largely through public payphones that usage takes place. And when this latter pattern of access is taken into account, even in rural areas of developing countries, the proportion of inhabitants that enjoy telephone use (albeit less conveniently than through private ownership) can be remarkably high.

Turning specifically to mobile phones, which are growing most rapidly in Africa, one has again to take into account the way in which these products are used in developing countries. Specifically, it appears that even in the poorest locations, there is a considerable amount of sharing mobile phones. One estimate cited in support of this contention is that 97 per cent of Tanzanians claim to have access to mobile telephony. For a recent estimate see James (2016).

Human skills

Both indicators of human skills adopted in the TAI suffer from the same weakness that was described above in relation to the Internet indicator, namely, that they say nothing about actual achievements derived from these educational 'inputs'. For, in just the same way that a given commodity or technology can have widely different effects, depending, among other things, on how they are used, so too may a certain number of school years endow different individuals with very different 'functionings' (a term owed to Sen, 1985).

Data compiled by IEA (2011) (The International Association for Educational Achievement, Trends in International Mathematics and Science Study [TIMMS], Boston College), for example, reveal that even among OECD countries there are quite striking differences in mathematical and scientific achievements at both the fourth- and eighth-grade levels. For developing countries, data are collected primarily by the UNESCO-UNICEF Monitoring Learning Achievement (MLA) project, which also focuses on the fourth and eighth grades. At the former level, the project covers mainly African countries and deals with three dimensions of educational achievement, namely, literacy, numeracy and life skills. Table 10.2 shows how a sample of nine sub-Saharan countries score on each of these dimensions. That is, it shows for each country what percentage of grade 4 pupils attained a specified minimum level of mastery in literacy and life skills. It does not show what an acceptable percentage for each subject in each country actually is.

Because similarly widespread inter-country disparities in learning achievements are apparent also at the eighth-grade level in the same country sample, the number of years in school appears to be a very weak indicator of technological capabilities. And unless this discrepancy is widely recognised by policymakers, there is a real danger that they will be inclined to focus their attention on

Table 10.2 Percentage of grade 4 pupils who attained the minimum level of mastery learning, selected African countries,* 1999

Country	Literacy	Numeracy	Life skills	Combined
Botswana	46.2	55.4	71.8	57.8
Madagascar	56.9	34.4	97.3	66.1
Malawi	15.3	30.7	95.4	54.9
Mali	50.4	37.9	69.8	54.4
Mauritius	77.6	70.3	71.6	70.3
Niger	39.3	15.3	44.9	25.6
Senegal	45.6	22.9	36.3	31.2
Uganda	64.3	41.9	78.8	54.4
Zambia	37.8	19.9	49.0	31.9

Source: Chinapah, 2003.
*Minimum mastery levels were established for each of the three learning achievements above, in the MLAI survey, which covered grades 4 and 5 for 48 countries. That document also defines the three dimensions of learning contained in the table.

increasing the quantity of, rather than the achievements derived from, education in schools. For many developing countries, there is already a tradition of favouring easily measurable education targets. In *Asian Drama*, for example, Myrdal (1968, vol. III:1657) observed,

> There has been a tendency in all the South Asian countries to think primarily in terms of quantitative targets such as the number of pupils enrolled in a certain category of schools, and less often in terms of qualitative improvements.

Because it is also stated in terms of educational 'inputs' rather than outputs or achievements, the second indicator used by the TAI to reflect skills – the gross tertiary science enrolment ratio – is subject to much the same criticism that has already been levelled against the first indicator (although, arguably, at such a relatively advanced stage of education, variations in achievements may be less pronounced than they appear to be at earlier stages). This second indicator, however, does run into the problem that, for many of the poorest African countries, the numbers of students enrolling in science at university are dismally low (partly, perhaps, because of the high costs involved and partly because of the colonial heritage). As such, this indicator, in common with several others I have considered, lacks almost any ability to discriminate among a large number of African countries, in spite of the fact that it is precisely these countries whose technological capabilities most urgently need to be assessed and improved upon. In fact, it is to this particular statistical problem associated with the TAI that I now turn.

The statistical manifestation of developed-country bias

In its 2001 index, only 72 countries were ranked by the TAI. For the unranked majority, 'data were missing or unsatisfactory for one or more indicators' (UNDP, 2001:46). It is true that data gaps occur for at least some countries on every indicator, except Internet hosts, for which the International Telecommunications Union maintains a very thorough database. Yet, it is very clear that data gaps are easily the most prevalent among two indicators chosen to reflect technology creation, namely, patents and royalty/license fees. Since the creation of technology is, as emphasised above, the most egregiously irrelevant concept for the vast number of African developing countries, it is scarcely surprising that the excluded group of countries is primarily drawn from the same country grouping. The point to be made here is not that there are overlooked or otherwise unrecorded data; it is rather that in the vast majority of cases, there simply are no patents or royalties to speak of. Thus it is that by excluding such a large number of countries the TAI has seemingly negated the very ideals that were set for it, namely, that it should 'be useful for developing countries' and that it 'must be able to discriminate between countries at the lower end of the range' of technological development. An index obviously cannot meet such demands if it is constructed in such a way as to exclude precisely the units that are meant to be studied.

For developing countries that are not excluded from the TAI on the grounds of data unavailability, let us examine how useful and discriminatory are the estimates for indicators that I have argued to be the most biased in favour of developed countries. These are the indicators pertaining to technology creation, Internet hosts and gross tertiary science enrolment ratios. (Other indicators were also subject to severe criticism but from a different standpoint.) Table 10.3 presents the values assigned to these indicators for the lowest ten (developing) countries in the index (six of which are African).

With the exception of two entries for Nicaragua, the only Latin American country in the group, the *t*-values are generally very low, as predicted. As such, these entries are not statistically different from the mean of each column, and they provide no extra information beyond those numbers.

Table 10.3 TAI scores on selected indicators, bottom ten countries

Country	Patents granted to residents	Receipts of royalties and licence fees	Internet hosts	Gross tertiary science enrolment ratio
India	1	(.)	0.1	1.7
Nicaragua	n/a	n/a	0.4	3.8
Pakistan	n/a	(.)	0.1	1.4
Senegal	n/a	0	0.2	0.5

(continued)

Table 10.3 Continued

Country	Patents granted to residents	Receipts of royalties and licence fees	Internet hosts	Gross tertiary science enrolment ratio
Ghana	(.)	n/a	(.)	0.4
Kenya	(.)	(.)	0.2	0.7
Nepal	n/a	0	0.1	0.7
Tanzania	n/a	(.)	(.)	0.2
Sudan	n/a	0	0	0.7
Mozambique	n/a	n/a	(.)	0.2
		t-values		
India	1.155	0	-0.078	0.635
Nicaragua			2.254★	2.542★
Pakistan		0	-0.078	0.363
Senegal		0	0.699	-0.454
Ghana	-0.577		-0.855	-0.545
Kenya	-0.577	0	0.699	-0.272
Nepal		0	-0.078	-0.272
Tanzania		0	-0.855	-0.726
Sudan		0	-0.855	-0.545
Mozambique			-0.855	-0.726

Source: UNDP, 2001 for top part of table.
★Significant at 95% level.
Note: Where entries in the TAI are designated as being less than half the unit shown. I have assigned them a value of zero. The TAI for 2009 contains more recent data but the conclusions remain largely the same (Nasir et al., 2011), as regards the countries mentioned in the table.

Revising the TAI

As I have described it, the major problem with the TAI is that because of its pronounced developed-country/urban bias, in many dimensions it excludes the vast majority of developing countries, and, even for the poor countries that are included, the scores that are recorded in those crucial dimensions are not significantly different from the mean. It seems clear, therefore, that the TAI does not even come close to meeting its stated goals of being useful to all developing countries and being able to discriminate among even the technologically most backward of those countries (most of which are in Africa). It seems equally clear, by symmetrical reasoning, that in order to redress these problems the developed country bias that so pervades the index needs to become much less pronounced.

Most important, the capability to innovate as measured by patents and royalties needs to be replaced by a concept that embraces a more general process of learning at earlier phases of acquisition of technological capabilities (earlier, that is to say, than the capability to innovate in the sense used in the TAI). As part of this more general process of learning, one would want to include, among other things, the increases in capabilities that emerge from the use of (new) technologies, the adaptations of such technologies to local circumstances (that are sometimes referred to as 'minor innovations') and the cumulative effects of these processes over time. The idea, then, is to capture increases in knowledge gained in a particular country rather than just the part that give rise to innovations. And what probably best reflects the outcomes of these gains in knowledge is the change in total factor productivity (that is, the component of growth that cannot be accounted for by the growth of physical and human capital).[5]

Fortunately, there is now at least one data set that contains information on changes in total factor productivity for a wide range of developed and developing countries. In particular, Steven Baier et al. (2002) have compiled data on this topic for 145 countries, using 10 years as a minimum period of observation. More recent data have been compiled for the period 1999 to 2014 by the Conference Board (2015). While it is, of course, true that total factor productivity includes more than just knowledge (resource allocation and economies of scale being just two such additional factors), the data now emerging on the topic seem to be far superior to the highly limited focus on technology creation in the TAI.

Developed-country bias was also found to be at work in the choice of indicators that measure just the number of different modes of communication. In particular, the indicators for Internet hosts and telephones assume that access to these 'new' and 'old' innovations occurs in the same way (namely, through individual ownership) in both developed and developing countries. Yet, I was at pains to show that, in at least the rural areas of developing countries, the Internet and fixed-line telephones (which often take the form of payphones) are shared among large numbers of (often poor) inhabitants, who, personally, own neither of these modes of communications (and although I did not single out mobile phones, the same pattern of gaining access to their services via sharing seems to be no less widespread). Ideally, therefore, a revised TAI would capture access to, rather than ownership of, these various technologies. And indeed, for some countries access measures do exist. At this stage, however, it seems unrealistic to rely on access rather than ownership data across a wide range of developing countries. With regard to fixed-line telephones, an imperfect but nonetheless useful proxy for the extent of communal sharing would be the number of payphones per country (data that are available from the ITU). This variable would go at least part of the way toward offsetting the pronounced degree of developed-country bias that currently besets the indicators now used by the TAI with respect to the Internet and telephones. Data gathered by Research ICT Africa on mobile phone sharing in a sample of African countries will also help in this respect (Research ICT Africa, 2011).

Partly because it is an indicator that is pitched at too high a level for many of the poorest developing counties (in Africa and South Asia), the lack of data on tertiary science enrolment ratios helps to exclude these countries from the ranking. By pitching this indicator at the lower level of science graduates from high school, more data will be available, and the problem of exclusion will be ameliorated. This too can be regarded as a means of offsetting the developed-country bias in the selection of indicators for the TAI.

The last line of criticism that was levelled at the TAI had to do with the distinction between the availability of commodities, technologies and schooling, on the one hand, and the achievements that are actually derived therefrom, on the other. With reference to the Internet and the number of years in school, I showed that there can be a vast difference between the potential available gains and the actual benefits that are realised in practice. It is of course the latter concept that better reflects technological capabilities, but it is often far more difficult to measure than the former. In the case of the Internet, though one might have expected to find a substantial body of research on the gains derived from this technology in different countries, in reality one can point to only a few such studies in the context of developing countries (one of which was described in relation to Table 10.2). As regards education, however, the situation is much more promising, in that concerted international efforts are under way to measure, among other things, the scientific achievements of students at the same level. The most extensive of these efforts is the *Trends In International Mathematics and Science Study*, which compares achievement across 46 countries drawn from developed, developing and 'transitional' regions. For the 2011 study, the number of participating countries amounted to 60, at which time there was more scope for including achievements in cross-country indices.

Probably the most important of the supplementary indicators, however, is the number of secondary school students per capita in Africa who receive vocational training. One of the reasons why it is so important is that according to Lall (1992:117), secondary education is '[t]he most critical input for industrial development.' Another reason is that the measure includes the majority of African countries, thus allowing discrimination between even the poorest countries in the world.

The relevant data are presented in Table 10.4, the last of whose columns shows the number of those receiving vocational training at secondary school as a percentage of the total population. Angola, Cameroon and The Democratic Republic of the Congo receive the highest scores, for reasons that are not immediately evident (though Cameroon has achieved some degree of success in industrialisation).

At a lower level, literacy is also linked to basic capabilities and can usefully discriminate among very low-income African countries. It should therefore also form part of an index designed for those specific countries.

Table 10.4. Percentage of secondary students with vocational training, Africa (available years)

Country	Year	Number with vocational training at secondary school	Population	Col. 3 ÷ by col. 4 in %
Angola	2011	400,265	21,942,296	1.8
Benin	2011	24,626	9,779,391	0.25
Burkina Faso	2013	29,730	17,084,554	0.17
Burundi	2013	26,149	10,465,959	0.25
Cameroon	2013	383,539	22,211,166	1.7
CAR	2012	3,850	4,619,500	0.08
Chad	2012	6,855	12,715,465	0.05
Democratic Republic of Congo	2013	745,343	72,522,861	1.0
Rep. Congo	2012	34,336	4,286,188	0.8
Côte d'Ivoire	2013	29,595	21,622,490	0.14
Djibouti	2013	2.338	864,554	0.27
Eritrea	2013	2,470	5,110,444	0.05
Ethiopia	2012	201,142	92,191,211	0.2
Ghana	2013	61,496	26,164,432	0.2
Lesotho	2012	6,691	2,057,331	0.33
Liberia	2011	17,565	4,079,574	0.4
Madagascar	2013	50,724	22,924,557	0.22
Malawi	2012	0	15,700,436	0
Mali	2013	109,899	16,592,097	0.66
Mauritania	2013	2,139	3,872,684	0.06
Mauritius	2012	11,446	1,258,653	0.9
Mozambique	2013	35,397	26,467,180	0.13

(continued)

Table 10.4 Continued

Country	Year	Number with vocational training at secondary school	Population	Col. 3 ÷ by col. 4 in %
Niger	2013	37,250	18,358,863	0.2
Rwanda	2013	80,458	11,078,095	0.7
Senegal	2011	37,516	13,357,003	0.28
Seychelles	2013	226	89,900	0.25
South Africa	2013	359,191	53,157,490	0.68
Sudan	2012	25,167	37,712,420	0.06
Swaziland	2011	0	1,212,458	0
Tanzania	2013	248,239	50,213,457	0.5
Togo	2011	27,573	6,566,179	0.4

Source: World Bank (2015) indicators.

Conclusions

It has long been recognised in institutional economics that technology is the driving force behind economic development, and this recognition has been confirmed by the empirical growth literature. Since then the role of technological capabilities in developing countries has been widely recognised. There is thus every reason to understand the technological features of countries at different stages of development.

Since 2000, a number of attempts have been made to construct indices of technological capabilities that include both developed and developing countries. (Because these indices are rather similar, not much is lost by focusing on just one of them, which for the purpose of this chapter is the Technology Achievement Index compiled by the UNDP.) These efforts are to be commended for seeking to collect comparable data over such a wide variety of countries. And the outcomes, as denoted by the values of the index, are certain to be of interest to countries such as Brazil and India, which are already quite heavily engaged in the type of technological activities in question. From the point of view of the majority of African developing countries, however, I have suggested that these measures are largely irrelevant, because they exhibit a pronounced degree of developed-country bias that translates, within such countries, into a bias in favour of the modern industrial sector (in a manner envisaged in the 1960s by Myrdal and Seers). I further suggest that the extent of this bias will tend to be larger the more that circumstances in the developing country differ from those in the rich. I find that the circumstances prevailing in the latter group of countries insert themselves into the new indices (with the TAI being used as the example thereof) in a number of different ways. One is by the choice of indicators (such as patents) that relate only to the most advanced of the developing countries (such as India and Brazil). Another takes place through a process described many years ago by Myrdal (1968), namely, of assuming that there are concepts which apply to all countries alike, regardless of how different the relevant goals, institutions, attitudes and other factors may actually be between rich and poor countries, and regardless of how far these differences invalidate the use of a certain concept in one context but not another. What these influences are shown to cause, is, among other things, that the TAI fails to achieve the very goals it itself sought to achieve, namely, to reflect the policy concerns of all countries, rich and poor alike, and to be useful for the latter.

I have suggested that one particular supplemental indicator be added to the TAI, namely, the number of secondary school students per capita who receive vocational training. It is especially important because secondary education is '[t]he most critical input for industrial development' (Lall, 1992:117), and also because it allows discrimination among some of the poorest countries in Africa. This indicator would also be important if an alternative approach was adopted, namely, one that eschewed measures such as the TAI and focused instead on those that dealt only with countries from Africa. Such an approach, which seems like an interesting and useful area for future research, would be forced to consider the capabilities that really matter to poor African countries, as opposed to those that are most relevant to rich, industrialised ones.

Notes

1 Archibugi and Coco (2005) have compared the various measures together with the TAI index, and to this end they compile a synopsis of the major features of the approaches in question. This

> shows at a glance that the various approaches contain significant similarities. In fact many indicators are identical, signalling the achievement of a certain consensus amongst scholars on what are the most significant components of technological capacity.
>
> (2005: 8, emphasis added)

All the approaches, for example, take

> the use of patents as an indicator of technology creation, … ICT indicators for technological infrastructures and diffusion; and tertiary education in science and engineering as an indicator of human skills.
>
> (Archibugi and Coco, 2005:15)

I argue below that these are precisely the indicators that are least relevant to the majority of developing countries, though one should recognise in this regard the inclusion in ArCo of a literacy variable, making it somewhat more reflective of developing-country circumstances.

2 As discussed in detail in the previous note.
3 The catch-up idea is most closely associated with Abramovitz (1986).
4 The UNDP (2001), for example, tends not to conclude from the unavailability of relevant data that more work should be devoted to the collection of such data.
5 The use of this well-known concept is apparently not even considered in the conception of the TAI. Note that not all increases in knowledge promote growth and some may do so indirectly rather than directly.

11 Conclusions

This book began by asking the question of whether sub-Saharan African countries can in the future generate 'a sufficient number of jobs at reasonable wages to *absorb* their rapidly growing populations into productive employment. In absolute magnitude, this challenge has no precedent in human history'[1] (Bloom & Freeman, 1987:106, emphasis in original). As a framework for answering the question, I have defended the use of a Lewis dual-economy model. Though this model has not worked at all well in the African context (Chapter 3), it does much to explain what happened in the history of the now developed countries, and it does still provide a useful basis both for understanding what has gone wrong in the Africa region as far as structural change is concerned and for explaining what might occur there in the future (Chapter 2).

Concern with future growth in the region, however, has tended to be muted by a fascination with the historically rapid growth record over the past 15 years or so. There has even been talk of a growth 'miracle' in recent years. But though such talk may represent an understandable reaction to the departure from many years of stagnant or even negative growth in the region, I have argued that talk of miracles is, at this stage, largely unwarranted. This for two reasons.

One is that in per capita terms – which are much more relevant to individual economic welfare than total values – African growth is far more modest in comparison with other developing regions (because of relatively rapid population growth). What is more, it is not at all clear that even this much more moderate growth can be sustained in the future (Chapter 4). The second reason why it is premature to talk of 'miracles' in Africa, is that for many countries in the region, growth in the past 15 years or so was driven by a boom in commodities rather than structural change of the kind Lewis envisaged, which almost all development economists regard as a sine qua non of progress to a developed country.

I analysed the sustainability[2] issue first with reference to the basic Lewis model, including (diagrammatically) both the labour supply and demand side determinants of the outcome (Chapter 3) and with reference also to the historical experience of the now developed countries and certain successful Asian developing nations. On the supply side of the labour market, the situation looks extremely daunting – for, in many coming decades, there will be a pronounced elongation of the labour supply curve in African countries due to rapid population growth. In particular, more than half the world's population growth between now and 2050 is expected to occur in Africa.

Note further that a rapid increase is projected to occur even if there is a sharp decrease in fertility levels in the near future: 'After 2050, Africa is expected to be the only major area still experiencing substantial population growth' (UN, 2015:3). To this already formidable problem, one should add the increase in the labour force that occurs when local products are displaced by cheap (Chinese) manufacturing imports (see below).

On the demand side, too, there is good reason for concern. Take the nature of technical change, which, for the now developed countries and the newly industrialising nations (NICs), was broadly neutral, with a constant capital-labour ratio, in the early stages of their structural transformation in favour of manufacturing (Chapter 2). African countries, by contrast, have been confronted with an increasingly labour-saving pattern of technical change, one that is likely to intensify over time as automation proceeds relentlessly, even in industries that are most resistant to it. For example, in relation to developed countries, it has been argued that

> garment production is extremely personnel dependent and therefore cost intensive. Robotic 3D assembly offers very interesting possibilities and potentials for high-tech and high-quality garment manufacturing with improved quality cost reduction and fast response to consumer market. The special robotic 3-dimensional (3D) sewing technology .... makes it possible for the first time to sew 3D seams automatically.[3]
>
> (Moll et al., 2009:9)

Then too, there is the small relative size of the modern sector in much of contemporary Africa, compared to the now-developed countries that were historically on the point of transforming their economies via structural change. This is a severe, albeit somewhat neglected, disadvantage for the Africa region, in as much as the formal sector of countries within it needs to grow that much faster to absorb increases in the labour supply and those already residing in the informal sector, whose numbers are often further swollen by the displacement of low-cost manufactured imports from China and other emerging economies, as just noted.

When the supply and demand sides are brought together, in what I describe as an extreme historical case, it becomes clear, from even some crude estimates, how daunting will tend to be the future employment prospects for Africa and by extension the prospects there for future poverty and inequality (Chapter 4). We know, for example, that in many African countries the formal sector constitutes not much more than 10 to 20 per cent of the total labour force, while the supply of labour is growing at around 2.7 per cent annually.

This means that the demand for labour by the formal sector will need to grow at between 15 and 30 per cent, just to absorb the new entrants to the labour force, let alone those who are already underemployed in the informal sector. Plainly, much more is required of the former sector than was the case when today's developed countries were at an equivalent stage in their development, when supply and demand circumstances were both more favourable (Chapter 2).

Especially since existing rates of underemployment in Africa are already substantial, one is bound to wonder what the future socio-political consequences of a limited demand and an ongoing high rate of population growth might be. After all, apart from one or two exceptions, there are few signs of a demand increase on anything like the scale that is needed. On the supply side, what is perhaps most alarming is the projected growth of youth un- and underemployment. For example, the African Economic Outlook (2012) forecasts that the number of young people in Africa will double by 2045. This, I should emphasise, would come on top of an already precarious situation, where 72 per cent of the youth population live on less than $2 per day.[4] Indeed, '[a] lack of sufficient job creation is by far the biggest hurdle young Africans face today' (African Economic Outlook, 2012).

It is also worthwhile to note the related fact that, according to Beegle et al. (2016), the absolute number of poor in Africa rose from 280 million persons in 1990 to 330 million in 2012. Consider, finally, that even if sufficient jobs *were* to be made available, it is not at all clear that the rising numbers of youth would be able to take them. For,

> It is estimated that about 133 million young people (more than 50 per cent of the youth population) in Africa are illiterate. Many young people have little or no skills and are therefore largely excluded from productive economic and social life. Those that have some education often exhibit skills irrelevant to current demand in the labour market, in a situation where education and skills requirements are increasing, resulting in millions of unemployed and underemployed youth.
>
> (African Economic Outlook, 2012)

Chapter 4 investigated the possible implications of these tendencies for future crime and violence in the region. It was taken as striking, in this regard, that Beegle et al. (2016) have observed an increase in the number of violent crimes since 2010. It is my hypothesis that this tendency will continue and probably worsen in the future, since there were shown to be links between (youth) un- and underemployment, income distribution/poverty and violent crime in the developing world, including Africa (though the relevant empirical evidence tends admittedly to be correlative rather than causal). On the one hand, that is to say, labour income is a primary determinant of poverty and inequality in developing countries, while these two variables in turn influence the degree of violent crime that is experienced (as measured, for example, by the number of homicides).

To this bleak picture, however, one needs to add a set of potentially countervailing tendencies, which together make up the second part of the book. Chapter 5, for example, discusses the potential afforded by an increase in the demand for labour in the African manufacturing sector. In particular, I dealt there with the following related areas: first, altering the choice of manufacturing branch in favour of those (such as garments) that are relatively labour-intensive (and efficient); second, changing the choice of technology in any given branch in the same direction and finally, changing the composition of units (Stewart et al., 1992) within any chosen branch towards appropriate technology, using small-scale firms with the potential to grow in terms of employment and productivity. I showed in each case that there appears to be considerable scope for employment creation, which in at least one country, Ethiopia, has already been partly realised. For sub-Saharan Africa as a whole, research from the 1980s suggested that more than a million extra jobs could be created by the choice of labour versus large-scale and capital-intensive technologies in manufacturing (efficiency would increase as well). But I was also at pains to emphasise the severe difficulties that will attend any attempts to exploit these countervailing tendencies. Not the least of such difficulties will be the need to recognise the central importance of technology in policymaking for employment creation and the need for a seriousness of purpose in such endeavours that has rarely been forthcoming in African industry.[5]

The next chapter (Chapter 6) had to do with the potential for increased labour demand that has emerged in the form of a new world order[6] since Lewis wrote his 1954 and 1979 articles. I discussed, in particular, four mechanisms through which global change may have affected the basic dual-economy model, namely, R&D, trade, FDI and aid. In each case, there has been a quite striking increase in the share of developing countries, especially, but not only, China and India.

In the case of global R&D, for example, the share of developing countries in the total has risen from 2 to 20 per cent over the past 40 years or so. I argued that this shift would possibly produce a higher share than before of developing country products and processes that are more relevant to the poor than the rich countries. The point is that preferences tend to be related to incomes, and countries with similar incomes will usually have similar preferences (though, as noted in Chapter 8, there are some potentially telling barriers to the unfettered working of the underlying induced innovation theory).

On the technological side, the new order may thus have produced a wider range of relatively labour-intensive methods than were formerly available and to this extent may have taken some of the pressure off the acute demand-side requirements of the Lewis model that were described in Part I above (though the hard evidence in support of, or against, this view is relatively scant). Accompanying these techniques will often have been low-cost, appropriate products, which serve to increase the consumer surplus for many of those living in poor, African countries. On the other hand, there have also been many cases in which the manufacturing branch in question (e.g., textiles) has been decimated due to competition from low-cost Chinese imports. This has a retarding influence on the pace of change in the Lewis model, because the displaced workers need to find alternative jobs. The net effect of the two mechanisms described in this paragraph is of course difficult to gauge with any degree of accuracy, though it is an issue well deserving of future research.

What does seem clear from the stagnant or even declining share of manufactures in total African output and exports, however, is that the new global economic order has in general done little to facilitate the type of structural change envisaged in that model. Yet, the reader also needs to bear in mind that certain services are included in the formal sector of the model and that according to some observers they can – and to some extent already have – begun to replace manufactures as the instrument of major economic change in Africa.

Ghani and O'Connell (2014), for example, are not alone in emphasising that today's services comprise not just traditional activities such as retailing, but also those based on IT, such as BPO (business process outsourcing) and call centres. 'The core of the argument', they aver, is that as the services produced and traded across the world expand with globalization, the possibilities for low-income countries to develop based on their comparative advantage expand. That comparative advantage can just as easily be in services as in manufacturing.

(2014:3)

These authors also point out that services have grown more rapidly than manufactures in the past decade in most African countries.

It is true that there is some merit in these claims. But it is equally true that there are several important problems with them. One such problem is that in the two African countries with arguably the most serious commitment to IT – Kenya and Rwanda – the predicted comparative advantage in modern services largely failed to materialise (see Chapter 6). Apparently, it is not necessarily easier to achieve an internationally competitive position in IT-based services than it is in light manufacturing. In fact, given the particular skill requirements of the former (see below), it may well be even more difficult. Then there is the question of how to interpret the evidence that services have generally grown faster than manufacturing in Africa. Some authors tend to infer something normative from this outcome, when it should often be seen, rather, in purely positive terms (in terms, that is to say, of what *is*, rather than something that is *desirable*).

In many cases, for example, the services sector has been unduly encouraged by policy (towards IT, for example), while manufacturing has been unduly neglected, as I believe is largely the case with light manufacturing. In such a situation there is nothing sacrosanct about the status quo. With more appropriate sectoral policy, manufacturing might in fact have done much better than services. Then, lastly, there is the difficult problem of skills. High productivity services tend, as numerous authors have pointed out, to be demanding of precisely the skills that are least abundant in the region. Rodrik, for example, argues,

> The classic case is information technology, which is a modern, tradable service. Long years of education and institution building are required before farm workers can be transformed into programmers or even call center operators. Contrast this with manufacturing where little more than manual dexterity is required to turn a farmer into a production worker in garments or shoes, raising his/her productivity by a factor of two or three.
>
> (Rodrik, 2014:13)

It is partly for this reason that Rodrik adopts a cautious view of the likelihood that African growth in the future will be much faster than it is now (though he does regard present rates as sustainable subject to the absence of major external shocks). The problem, though, is that current rates of growth are not, as noted above, anything like miraculous in per capita terms, and if indeed they do persist in the future, this will take place in what, from a dual-economy perspective, is a deteriorating context (if, that is, nothing major is done to change the status quo with respect to employment generation). And one will then, more than ever, be at socio-political risk from the problems of un(der)employment, poverty and inequality, as described in Chapter 4. Indeed, from these points of view, an extrapolation of the present situation into the future may well not be sustainable, as there may be socio-political unrest on a scale that impinges on the macro economy.

Yet, following Rodrik (2014), one cannot entirely deny the possibility that the future may not look at all like the present. 'Perhaps', he suggests, 'Africa will be the breeding ground of new technologies that will revolutionize services for broad masses and do so in a way that creates high-wage jobs for all' (Rodrik, 2014:13). In the short to medium run, however, such a scenario seems to me rather unlikely, for African countries are generally lacking in the type of innovative capabilities that would be required for the purpose (South Africa and Kenya are perhaps partial exceptions in this regard). What is more, high productivity services are unlikely to create the millions of jobs that are required in the region to stave off the undesirable socio-political consequences I described in Chapter 4. In any event, there is clearly considerable scope for research designed to investigate the feasibility of a development strategy in which IT and other services at some point take over the role formerly played by manufacturing in the history of the now developed countries and countries that are approaching such status. At present the evidence required for such an assessment is sorely lacking.

The two chapters in the third and final part of the book (Chapters 9 and 10) dealt with technological capabilities and to some extent also with the choice of technology (note here that the acquisition of the former also tends to influence the latter). Both areas have suffered from considerable neglect in the past 15 years, even though research conducted in the 1970s and 1980s had established that there were acute problems with technology in Africa's industrial strategy.[7] The choice of technology, for example, once a major policy issue, has all but disappeared from research and policy agendas, even though the early research had indicated that the problems in the area had not been mitigated to any substantial degree. Moreover, as indicated in Chapters 6 and 8, there are now new issues to be addressed, such as whether China and India tend to generate more appropriate technology than do the developed countries in the same manufacturing branches. Some authors, for example, suggest that this is true at least with respect to private Chinese FDI in Africa, but far more research is needed.

At the heart of this debate is the induced innovation model, which posits that countries with a relative scarcity of capital and an abundance of labour are more likely to generate appropriate forms of technology than countries with something approaching the opposite set of factor endowments. A substantial and pertinent research agenda awaits those who are willing to address themselves empirically to the question. In part, the suggested research can follow the methods adopted by studies from the 1970s and 1980s that were designed to test whether foreign investment from developing countries produces more appropriate technologies than investment from the developed world (for some of the results and supportive evidence, see the literature cited in Chapter 6).

It bears reiterating here that the choice of technology is not the only factor that determines the shape and position of the demand curve for labour in the Lewis model. For what is also important is the selection of the manufacturing branch. Data reported in Chapter 5, for example, showed that there can be marked differences between different branches in terms of their labour-intensities. Garments, for example, are by far the most promising in this regard and require relatively few skills. They warrant serious consideration as a priority sector in future policy towards trade and industry. Kenya and Lesotho, for example, already have nascent garment industries that show promise, and Madagascar was historically a major exporter of these products based partly on FDI.[8] According to McKinsey & Co. (2015), 'For the first time in our survey, African nations appear on the list of countries expected to play more important roles in apparel manufacturing'.

Chapter 9 dealt partly with the choice of technology in African manufacturing and focused in part on a paradox that has long puzzled researchers in the area, namely, of why firms are apt to choose large-scale, capital- and import-intensive technologies when more appropriate and profitable alternatives are available. Indeed, as noted above, earlier research indicates that the choice of the latter over the former can result in more than a million extra jobs in African manufacturing as a whole. My hypothesis here was that the issue has thus far been largely miscast as the choice between one large-scale capital intensive plant versus a smaller, more labour-intensive alternative. In reality, however, the choice is more likely to be between one large-scale plant and a *number* of smaller, more labour-intensive ones. These, however, require entrepreneurial and managerial resources which are not readily forthcoming in most poor, African countries (the choice of technology, that is to say, is better described in three rather than only two dimensions, as shown in the diagrams in Chapter 9).

In Hirschman's terms there are traits (capabilities) which need to be 'made', a process which requires certain latitudes in design and a time period for development that is quite a bit longer than is usually thought to be necessary. The process of trait-making was illustrated partly with reference to labour-intensive road construction projects in Africa, some of which have turned out to be very successful in relation to employment creation (e.g., in Kenya). Some of the lessons from those projects are likely to carry over to manufacturing as well, such as the need to decentralise state power to the level at which those projects are actually administered.

The role of the state also promises to be crucial in the exploitation of new markets for labour-intensive manufactures that will be created, as Chinese trade shifts in the way noted above, towards higher value-added sectors and branches as unskilled wages rise fairly sharply. I am thinking here for example of all the trait-making activities engaged in by the state in Ethiopia, the site of some of Africa's most successful EPZs, such as the provision of roads, electricity, finance and so on. Indeed, the strenuous efforts made by that country to attract and retain FDI in manufacturing stand as a lesson to other countries in the region, whose endeavours in this regard seem altogether more halfhearted.

I dealt again in Chapter 10 with the subject of technological capabilities, which received extensive treatment in the 1980s and 1990s, but which, like other related technology concepts, has unfortunately tended to recede from view in the more recent literature on and policy towards African industry. My concern, however, was not to review, or even to summarise, this very broad body of literature. Rather, it was to focus on the disconnect that exists between the micro studies on the one hand and, on the other hand, the attempts that have been made at the macro level to measure the technological capabilities of an entire country. Using as a framework the ideas of institutional economics and the TAI (Technology Achievements Index) from the UNDP as an example of such an index, I found evidence of a pronounced developed-country bias, which effectively excludes most African countries and many of the most salient capabilities in the manufacturing sector of these countries (especially for relatively small-scale firms).

The ability to adapt imported technology, for example, is one of the most prevalent and essential capabilities in developing countries such as those in Africa, but it is not captured in any way by the index, which focuses instead mainly on capabilities that are relevant to developed countries, such as the creation of entirely new technology. What I suggested as an alternative, therefore, was the creation of an index which covers only African countries and contains more relevant indicators, such as the percentage of secondary school students receiving vocational training (data on which are now available for African countries from the World Bank). Such an index should also be capable of tracing the development – improvement or deterioration – of relevant capabilities over time. For, as things now stand, there are few sources that can tell us how capabilities that are relevant to Africa have evolved over time.[9]

Note, relatedly, that I have not yet addressed the potential role of small-scale firms in a revised labour-intensive industrial strategy. Such potential, it is true, is not apparent from the original (1954) Lewis article in which these firms belong to the informal sector, whose only task is to act as a reservoir of cheap labour for a dynamic formal sector. In his later, 1979 article, however, Lewis seemed to suggest a more positive role for the small-scale sector, when he observed, 'Small scale firms are more likely to use appropriate technology, and will provide more employment per unit of capital than large firms, so they are much to be cherished' (Lewis, 1979:223). It is not clear though what specific policies he thought should be applied to the informal sector.

Some authors have argued in this regard that there are many heavy biases against small-scale firms in African manufacturing.[10] And some among them further suggest,

> Structured markets are needed: this means reserving a proportion of resources-credit, foreign exchange and so on – for the small-scale sector and thus ensuring that a "market" solution generates adequate resources for the sector. Structured markets of this kind were successful in securing resources for the small-scale sector in India.
>
> (Stewart et al., 1992:26)[11]

Other authors, however (such as Diao et al., 2016), maintain that this policy can be criticised as being indiscriminate: it promotes both efficient and inefficient small-scale firms. The task, as they see it, should be to promote only the former.

Indeed, basing their results on a detailed firm-level survey in Tanzania, Diao et al. (2016) are able to identify a set of enterprises that is both efficient and employment-intensive, and which deserves better (or more consistent) treatment than is currently being meted out to it by the institutions of the state. How best to promote these firms is not yet clear,[12] but one possibility is via 'plug and play' industrial parks, which have been used to great effect in China in allowing dynamic small-scale firms to expand into much larger entities. Indeed, 'the parks have enabled many Chinese SMEs to grow from family operations focused on domestic markets into global powerhouses' (Dinh & Hang, 2014:44). This was achieved mainly by offering the firms in question

> good basic infrastructure (e.g. roads, energy, water and sewage), security, stream-lined government regulations (e.g. government service centers) and affordable industrial land, they also provided technical training, low cost standardized factory shells allowing Chinese entrepreneurs to "Plug and Play" as well as Chinese workers with free and decent housing accommodations right next to the plants.
> (Dinh et al., 2012)

Whether such zones would also benefit Africa's small-scale enterprises remains very much to be seen, but what is clear is that it would require far more commitment by the state to supply the necessary inputs than has generally been forthcoming, in the region.

I conclude by returning to the question posed in the title of this book, namely, of whether current African growth is sustainable. Prima facie, it may seem as if continued growth of around 2 per cent per annum per head is not too demanding a requirement (apart from the recent fall in commodity prices). But that would be to ignore the fragility of the current socio-political situation in the region, which is *already* based on an unusually large amount of un(der)employment, growing numbers in poverty and high inequality (especially in Southern Africa). Continuation of the existing development model, with its emphasis on large-scale, capital-intensive endeavours, would only worsen these problems and heighten the associated risks of further socio-political instability. In effect, therefore, sustainability requires a very different pattern of development, one that is based on the policies and opportunities suggested in the previous chapters, especially those that foster employment creation, such as the supply of labour-intensive products to markets formerly supplied by the Chinese. I have emphasised the technological aspects of such policies because they seem to me especially salient and relatively neglected. But there are of course other areas that need to be explored as well, such as the workings of labour markets in African industry.

In short, what this book has proposed is to see technology in Africa not just as a micro-economic choice problem, but as one that encompasses technological capabilities and small-scale firms and is viewed as the core of an entire alternative development strategy, which involves sectors and macro-economic policymaking (towards, for example, foreign exchange rates). And to this end, there should be a focus of interest in academic and policy circles of research that was mentioned in the chapters above (including the issues raised by the appearance of a new global economic order which has seen the emergence and growth of China, India and some other developing countries). Could it be, for example, that these countries are associated with more appropriate products and processes than those from developed countries? Or do their lower prices reflect instead mainly low-quality or counterfeit products and processes? Answers to these and other questions will help to determine the welfare effects of the new global order on producers and consumers in African countries.

What also needs to be carefully studied from a future research point of view is the forthcoming study by the McKinsey Global Research Institute, entitled *Lions on the Move II*. In particular, a prepublication summary of that publication makes some major claims about future manufacturing, output and employment in Africa. For example, it alleges:

> Africa could nearly double its manufacturing output to $930 billion in 2025 from $500 billion today, provided countries take decisive action to create an improved environment for manufacturers. Three-quarters of that potential could come from Africa-based companies meeting domestic demand; today, Africa imports one-third of the food, beverages, and other similar processed goods it consumes. The other one-quarter could come from more exports. The rewards of accelerated industrialization would include a step change in productivity and the creation of up to 14 million stable jobs over the next decade.
>
> (McKinsey Global Institute, 2016)

It will be instructive to learn from the forthcoming report how these particular figures are arrived at. For example, the strategy seems to rely to quite a large extent on import substitution, though such a policy does not have a favourable legacy in most developing countries. What exactly constitutes an 'improved environment' for manufacturers? What type and extent of technological capabilities would be needed, and how could they be acquired?

Notes

1 So far, as the chapters below clearly indicate, Africa has significantly failed to meet this challenge.
2 'Sustainability' is used here in an economics rather than an environmental sense. And I emphasise the socio-political determinants of sustainability in this sense.
3 This, like automation before it, raises the spectre of comparable advantage 'reversal', whereby labour-saving technological progress in the developed countries robs developing countries of their comparative advantage based on cheap labour. See James (1994).
4 Though *rates* of poverty have fallen, on average.
5 In the text I cited the example of South Africa, which, despite suffering from unemployment of 25%, has shown little interest in pursuing a serious labour-intensive industrial policy (and despite much rhetoric to the contrary).
6 There is of course no official 'new order'; I use this term to summarise the major changes in global economic relations that have occurred in the past 20 years or so, especially as regards the position of the developing world.
7 See Stewart et al. (1992) for a full discussion, including some case studies of African manufacturing.
8 For an even earlier success story, see the case of Mauritius and more specifically the EPZs that were adopted in garment production. See Frankel (2010).
9 Even with existing composite indicators such as the TAI, it is difficult to monitor change in technological capabilities since the composition of the indexes is inclined to change.
10 See Stewart et al. (1992).
11 The Indian policy was, however, discontinued.
12 As a means of identifying promising young entrepreneurs, Diao et al. (2016) mention the competitions that have been held in countries such as Tanzania and Nigeria.

References

Abramovitz, M. (1986) 'Catching up, forging ahead, & falling behind', *Journal of Economic History*, 46,2:385–406.

ADBI (2011) 'Factor Market Distortions: An Alternative Hypothesis' working paper series, no. 279, Tokyo, Japan. Online: https://core.ac.uk/download/pdf/6284094.pdf?repositoryId=153 (accessed 12 August 2014).

African Development Bank (2014) *Data Portal*, Cote d'Ivoire, ADB.

African Economic Outlook (2012) *Promoting youth employment in Africa*. Online: www.africaneconomicout/look.org/en/theme.

Agnew, R. (2012) 'Reflection on "A Revised Strain Theory of Delinquency"', *Social Forces*, 91,1:33–38.

Amsden, A. (1977) 'The division of labor is limited by the type of market: the case of the Taiwanese machine tool industry', *World Development*, 5,3:217–233.

Archibugi, D. & Coco, A. (2005) 'Measuring technological capabilities at the country level: a survey & a menu for choice', *Research Policy*, 34:175–194.

Archibugi, D. & Coco, A. (2004) 'A new indicator of technological capabilities for developed and developing countries', *World Development* 32,4:629–654.

Bagachwa, M. (1992) 'Choice of technology in small & large firms: grain milling in Tanzania', *World Development*, 20:97–107.

Baier, S. Dwyer, G. & Tamura, R. (2002) 'How important are capital & total factor productivity for economic growth?' working paper no. 2002-2a, Federal Reserve Bank of Atlanta.

Baisser, C. (2011) 'Brief history of SEZs & overview of policy debates', in Farole, T. (ed.) *Special Economic Zones in Africa: Comparing Performance & Learning from Global Experience*, World Bank.

Barclay's Capital (2011) *China: Beyond the Miracle*. Online: http://www.fullertreacymoney.com/system/data/images/archive/2011-11-11/Barclays11-8-11-China-Beyond-the-Miracle.pdf (accessed 12 December 2014).

Baron, C. & van Ginneken, W. (1984) *Appropriate Products, Employment & Technology*, London: Macmillan.

Becker, G. (1968) 'Crime & punishment: an economic approach,' *Journal of Political Economy*, 76:169–190.

Beegle, K., Christiansen, L., Dabalen, A., & Gaddis, I. (2016) *Poverty in a Rising Africa*, Washington, D.C.: World Bank. © World Bank.

Berthelemy, J. (2011) 'China's engagement & aid effectiveness in Africa', African Development Bank Group, Working paper no. 129. Online: http://www.afdb.org/fileadmin/uploads/afdb/Documents/Publications/Working%20129.pdf.

Black, A. & Hasson, R. (2012) 'Capital-intensive industrialization & comparative advantage: can South Africa do better in labour demanding manufacturing?' Towards Carnegie III, conference held at the University of Cape Town, September.

Bloom, D. & Freeman, R. (1987) 'Poplulation growth, labor supply, & employment in developing countries', in D. Johnson & Lee, R. (eds.) *Population Growth & Economic Development: Issues & Evidence*, Madison: University of Wisconsin Press.

Boltho, A. and Weber, M. (2009) 'Did China follow the East Asian development model?', *European Journal of Comparative Economics*, 6,2:267–286.

Bourguignon, F. (1999) 'Crime as a social cost of poverty & inequality: a review focusing on developing countries', *Revista Desarrolo y Sociedad*, Universidad de los Andes, Colombia.

Bratton, M. & Rothschild, D. (1994) 'The institutional bases of governance in Africa', in Hyden, G., & Bratten, H. (eds.) *Governance & Politics in Africa*, Boulder: Lynne Rienner.

Burenstam Linder, S. (1961) *An Essay on Trade & Transformation*, Stockholm: Almqvist & Wicksell.

Cameron, A., Ewen, M. Ross-Degnan, D. Ball, D & Laing, R. (2009) 'Medicine prices, availability & affordability in 36 developing and middle-income countries: a secondary analysis', *Lancet*, 373:240–249.

Chandy, L. (2015) 'Why is the number of poor people in Africa increasing when Africa's economies are growing? Africa in Focus, Brookings, May 4. Online: http://www.brookings-edu/blogs/africa-in-focus/posts/2015/05/04 (accessed 13 January 2016).

Chenery, H. & Keesing, D. (1979) 'The changing composition of developing country exports', World Bank staff working paper, no. 314, Washington, D.C.

Chinapah, V. (2003) 'Monitoring learning achievement (MLA) in Africa', Association for the Development of Education in Africa, ADEA biennial meeting, Mauritius.

Clark, N. & Juma, C. (1990) 'Evolutionary theories in economic thought' in Dosi, G. (ed.) *Technical Change & Economic Theory*, London: Pinter.

Clark, W. (1978) *Socialist Development & Public Investment in Tanzania*, Toronto: Toronto University Press.

Clarke, G. (2012) 'Manufacturing firms in Africa: some stylized facts about wages & productivity', Munich Personal RePec Archive, no. 36122. Online: https://www.mpra.ub.uni-muenchen.de/36122/

Cling, J., Razafindrakoto, M. & Roubaad, F. (2007) 'Export processing zones in Madagascar', International Centre for Trade & Sustainable Development, Geneva.

Collier, P. (2000) 'Economic causes of civil conflict & their implications for policy', World Bank. Online: http://web.worldbank.org/archive/website01241/WEB/IMAGES/ECONONMI.pdf

Collier, P. & Hoeffler, A (2004) 'Greed & grievance in civil war', *Oxford Economic Papers*, 56,4:563–595.

Collier, P. & Hoeffler, A. (2000) 'On the incidence of civil war in Africa', Center for Development Research (ZEF), Bonn.

Conference Board, (2015) *Total Economy Database*. Online: https://www.conference-board.org/retrievefile.cfm?filename=The-Conference-Board-2015-Productivity-Brief-Summary-Tables-1999-2015.pdf&type=subsite (accessed 4 January, 2016).

Cramer, C. (2012) 'Unemployment & participation in violence'. Background paper for the World Development Report 2011, World Bank. Online: http://web.worldbank.org/archive/website01306/web/pdf/wdr%background%20paper%20-%20cramer.pdf (accessed 20 February, 2014).

Cypher, J. & Dietz, J. (2004) *The Process of Economic Development*, 2nd edn., London: Routledge.

Dahlman, C. & Westphal, L. (1982) 'Technical effort in industrial development – an interpretive survey of recent research', in Stewart, F. & James, J. (eds.) *The Economics of New Technology in Developing Countries*, London: Pinter.

De Veen, J. (1980) *The Rural Access Roads Programme*, Geneva: ILO.

Demombynes, G. & Özler, B. (2002) 'Crime & local inequality in South Africa', Policy Research Working Paper. World Bank. Online: http://dx.doi.org/10.1596/1813-9450-2925 (accessed 5 May, 2006).

Der-Petrossian, B. (1995) 'Importance of appropriate building codes & regulations in improving low-income settlements conditions in African region', UN Centre for Human Settlements, Nairobi.

Diao, X., Kweka, J. McMillan, M. & Qureshi, Z. (2016) 'Re-thinking African development strategies from the bottom up: macro & micro evidence from Tanzania', draft.

Dinh, H., Palmade, V., Chandra, V. & Cassar, F. (2012) *Light Manufacturing in Africa: Targeted Policies to Enhance Private Investment & Create Jobs*, World Bank/Africa Development Forum.

Dinh, H., Mishra, D., Duy, B. L., Minh, P. D., Pham, H., & Thu, T. (2014) *Light manufacturing in Vietnam: Creating jobs and prosperity in a middle-income economy*. Washington, DC: World Bank, online: http://documents.worldbank.org/curated/en/116451468126895451/Light-manufacturing-in-Vietnam-creating-jobs-and-prosperity-in-a-middle-income-economy.

Douglas, M. & Isherwood, B. (1979) *The World of Goods*, London: Allen Lane.

The Economist (2007, March 1) 'Soft drinks in China: orange gold'.

The Economist (2015a, 30 May) 'Neither a sprint nor a marathon'.

The Economist (2015b, 30 May) 'Made to measure'.

The Economist (2012, 23 July) 'The economics of crime: Is crime rational?'

The Economist (2013, May 27) 'Why does Kenya lead the world in mobile money?'.

Edmonds, G. & Howe, J. (1980) *Roads and Resources*, London: IT Publications.

Edmonds, G. & Ruud, O. (1984) *Labour-Based Construction and Maintenance: Some Indicators of Viability*, World Employment Programme Research, Geneva: ILO.

Edwards, L. & Jenkins, R. (2013) 'The impact of Chinese import penetration on the South African manufacturing sector', Southern Africa Labour & Development Research Unit Working Paper, no. 102. Cape Town: SALDRU, University of Cape Town.

Edwards, L. & Jenkins, R. (2015) 'The impact of Chinese import penetration on the South African manufacturing sector', *Journal of Development Studies*, 51:4, 447–63.

Eichengreen, P. and Gupta, P. (2011) 'The service sector as India's road to economic growth', Working Paper 16757. Cambridge, MA: The National Bureau of Economic Research.

Etta, F. (2002) 'The trouble with community telecentres'. Online: www.acacia.org.za/telecentres-etta.htm (accessed 5 September, 2006).

Etta, F. & Wamahiu, S. (2003) *Information & Communication Technologies for Development*, IDRC, Ottawa: Canada.

Farole, T. (2011) 'Special Economic Zones in Africa: Comparing Performance & Learning from Global Experiences', Washington, D.C.: World Bank.

Forsyth, D., McBain, N. and Solomon, R. (1982) 'Technical rigidity and appropriate technology', in Stewart, F. and James, J. (eds.) *The Economics of New Technology in Developing Countries*, London, Pinter.

Fox, L., Haines, C., Munoz, J. and Thomas, A. (2013) 'Africa's got work to do: employment prospects in the new century', IMF Working Paper, WP/13/201.

Frankel, J. (2010) 'Mauritius: African success story' NBER Working Paper Series, Number 16569. Online: http://www.nber.org/papers/w16569.pdf (accessed 8 March 2014).

Fransman, M. (1984) 'Some hypotheses regarding indigenous technological capability & the case of machine production in Hong Kong', in Fransman, M. & King, K. (eds.) *Technological Capability in the Third World*, New York: St. Martin's Press.

Garrity, M. & Picard, L. (1994) 'Institutional development revisited', in Picard, L. & Garrity, M. (eds.) *Policy Reform for Sustainable Development in Africa*, Boulder: Lynne Rienner.

Geiger, M. & Moller, L. (2015) *Fourth Ethiopia Economic Update: Overcoming Constraints in the Manufacturing Sector*, World Bank, working paper 97916.

Ghani, E. & O'Connell, S. (2014) 'Can service be a growth escalator in low income countries?' World Bank, Policy Research Working Paper, no. 6971.

Golub, S. & Hayat, F. (2014) 'Employment, unemployment and underemployment in Africa', Wider Working paper no. 14, Helsinki.

Green, R. (1978) 'The automated bakery: a study of decision taking, goals, processes & problems in Tanzania', Discussion Paper no. 141, *Institute of Development Studies*, University of Sussex.

Hanauer, L. & Morris, L. (2014) *Chinese Engagement in Africa: Drivers, Reactions, & Implications for US Policy*, Santa Monica, CA: Rand Corporation.

Hayami, Y. & Ruttan, V. (1987) 'Population growth and agricultural productivity' in Johnson, D. and Lee, R. (eds.) *Population Growth and Economic Development*, Madison: University of Wisconsin Press.

Heller, P. & Tait, A. (1983) 'Government employment & pay: some international comparisons', Occasional paper 24, Washington, D.C: IMF.

Helpman, E. (2004) *The Mystery of Economic Growth*, Cambride, MA: Belknap.

Hirschman, A. (1967) Development Projects Observed, Washington, D.C: Brookings.

Hirschman, A. & Rothschild, M. (1973) 'The changing tolerance for income inequality in the course of economic development', *Quarterly Journal of Economics*, 87,4:544–566.

Hughes, S. (2003) 'Community multimedia centres: creating digital opportunities for all' in Girard, B (ed.) *The One to Watch: Radio, New ICTs & Interactivity*, Rome: FAO

Hyman, E. (1993) 'Production of edible oils for the masses by the masses; the impact of the RAM press in Tanzania', *World Development*, 21:429–443.

ILO (2015) *World Employment & Social Outlook*, Geneva: ILO.

ILO (2014) *Global Employment Trends*, Geneva: ILO.

ILO (2013) *Inequality in Southern Africa, options for redress*, Policy brief. Online: http://www.ilo.org/actrav/WCMS_230181/lang--en/index.htm.

James, J. (2016) *The Impact of Mobile Phones on Poverty & Inequality in Developing Countries*, Heidelberg: Springer.

James, J. (2013) *Digital Interactions in Developing Countries: An Economic Perspective*, London: Routledge.

James, J. (2004) *Innovation Technology & Development*, London: Routledge.

James, J. (2000) *Consumption, Globalization and Development*, Basingstoke: Macmillan.

James, J. (1999) 'Trait-taking versus trait-making in technical choice: the case of Africa', *Journal of International Development*, 11,6: 797–810.

James, J. (1995). *The State, Technology & Industrialisation in Africa*, London: Macmillan.

James, J. (1994) 'Microelectronics & the Third World: an integrative survey of literature' in Cooper, C. (ed.) *Technology & Innovation in the International Economy*, Cheltenham: Edward Elgar.

James, J. (1989) *Improving Traditional Rural Technologies*, Basingstoke: Macmillan.

James, J. (1987) 'Population and Technical Change in the Manufacturing Sector of Developing Countries' in Johnson, D. and Lee, R. (eds.) *Population Growth and Economic Development*, Madison: University of Wisconsin Press.

James, J. (1982) 'Product standards in developing countries', in Stewart, F. & James, J. (eds.) *The Economics of New Technology in Developing Countries*, London: Frances Pinter.

James, J. (1977). 'Products, Processes and Incomes: Cotton Clothing in India', *World Development*, 4,2:143–149.

James, J. and Stewart, F. (1981). 'New Products: A Discussion of the Welfare Effects of the Introduction of New Products in Developing Countries', *Oxford Economic Papers*, 33,1:81–107.

Jauch, H. (2011) *Time to Turn the Tide*, Bonn, Germany: Friedrich Ebert Stiftung.

Jéquier, N & Hu, Y. (1989) *Banking and the Promotion of Technical Development*, London: Macmillan.

Jin, J. (2010) *Foreign Companies Accelerating R and D Activity in China*. Tokyo: Fujitsu Research Institute.

Johnston, B. & Kilby, P. (1975) *Agriculture & Structural Transformation*, Oxford: Oxford University Press.

Jones, G., & Rodgers, D. (2011) 'The World Bank's world development report 2011 on conflict, security & development', *Journal of International Development*, 23,7:980–995.

Kaplinksy, R. (2011) 'Schumacher meets Schumpeter: appropriate technology below the radar', *Research Policy*, 40,2:193–203.

Kaplinsky, R. (1990) *The Economies of Small*, London: IT Publications.

Kaplinsky, R. (1987) 'Appropriate technology in sugar manufacturing', in Stewart, F. (ed.) *Macro Policies for Appropriate Technology in Developing Countries*, Boulder: Westview.

Karnani, A. (2007) 'The Mirage of Marketing to the Bottom of the Pyramid: How the Private Sector Can Help Alleviate Poverty', *California Management Review*, 49,4:90–111.

Kauzya, J. (2007) *Political Decentralization in Africa: Experiences of Uganda, Rwanda & South Africa*, New York: UN. Online: http://unpan1.un.org/intradoc/groups/public/documents/un/unpan028411.pdf. (Accessed 2 May 2014).

Khan, H. & Thorbecke, E. (1989) 'Macroeconomic effects & diffusion of alternative technologies with a social accounting matrix framework: the case of Indonesia', *Journal of Policy Modelling*, 11,1:131–156.

Lall, S. (2005) 'Is African industry competing?' Queen Elizabeth House, Oxford, working paper no.121.

Lall, S. (1996) *Learning from the Asian Tigers*, London: Macmillan.

Lall, S. (1992) 'Structural problems of African industry', in Stewart, F., Lall, S & Wangwe, S. (eds.) *Alternative Development Strategies in Sub-Saharan Africa*, London: Macmillan.

Lall, S. & Pietrobelli, C. (2002) *Failing to Compete: Technology Development & Technology Systems in Africa*, Cheltenham: Edward Elgar.

Lancaster, K. (1966) 'A new approach to consumer theory', *Journal of Political Economy*, 74,2,132–157.

Landes, D. (1965) 'Japan & Europe: contrasts in industrialization', in Lockwood, D. (ed.) *The State & Economic Enterprise in Japan*, Princeton, N.J.: Princeton University Press.

Lecraw, D. (1977) 'Direct investment by firms from less developed countries', *Oxford Economic Papers*, 29,3:442–457.

Lewis, W.A. (1979) 'The dual economy revisited', *The Manchester School*, 47,3:211–229.

Lewis, W.A. (1954) 'Economic development with unlimited supplies of labour', *The Manchester School*, 2.2,2:139–191.

Mann, L., Graham, M. & Friederici, N. (2015) *The Internet & Business Processing Outsourcing in East Africa*, Oxford Internet Institute Report, Oxford, UK. Online: https://www.oii.ox.ac.uk/archive/downloads/publications/The_Internet_and_Business_Process_Outsourcing_in_East_Africa.pdf (accessed 3 April, 2016).

Manor, J. (1995) 'Democratic decentralization in Africa', *IDS Bulletin*, 26:81–88.

Martins, P. (2014) *Structural Change in Ethiopia: An Employment Perspective*, Policy research working paper no. 6749, Washington, D.C.: The World Bank.

Martins, P. (2013) 'Growth employment and poverty in Africa: tales of lions and cheetahs', Background paper for the World Development Report 2013, World Bank.

McCutcheon, R. (2008) *Labour-Intensive Construction & Maintenance in Sub-Saharan Africa: The World Bank Played a Critical Role During the 1970s & 1980s; What are the Prospects for the Future?* A paper for discussion at the World Bank, 7 April.

McCutcheon, R. (1995) 'Employment creation in public works', *Habitat International*, 19:331–355.

McCutcheon, R. & Parkins, F. (2009) *South Africa's Expanded Public Works Programme: a Case-Study in Government Sponsored Employment Creation & Poverty Alleviation Focusing Upon the Infrastructure Component*, online: http://www.robert-mccutcheon.com/resources/Newcastle%20CofFEE%2009%20RM%20FTP%20Paper%20as%20Published%20Dec09.pdf (accessed 18 July, 2011).

McKinsey Global Institute (2016) 'Realizing the potential of Africa's Economies'.

McKinsey & Co. (2015) 'East Africa: the next hub for apparel sourcing', Article. Online: http://www.mckinsey.com/industries/retail/our-insights/east-africa-the-next-hub-for-apparel-sourcing (accessed 23 April, 2016).

McMillan, M., Rodrik, D. & Verdusco-Gallo, I. (2014) 'Globalization, structural change, & productivity growth, with an update on Africa,' *World Development*, 63:11–32.

Moll, P., Schütte, U. & Zöll, K. (2009) 'Robotic 3d garment assembly & automation material handling; is it possible?' in Lutz, W., Kartsounis, G. & Carosio, S. (eds.) *Transforming Clothing Production into a Demand-Driven, Knowledge-Based, High-Tech Industry*, Heidelberg: Springer.

Myrdal, G. (1968) *Asian Drama*, New York: Pantheon.

Nasir, A., Ali, T. Shahdin, S. & Rahman, T. (2011) 'Technology achievement index 2009: ranking & comparative study of nations', *Scientometrics*, 87:41–62.

National Science Board (2014) *Science & Engineering Indicators*, Arlington, VA: National Science Foundation (NSB 14-01).

Nattrass, N. (2003) 'Unemployment & AIDs: the social-democratic challenge for South Africa', Centre for Social Science Research, University of Cape Town, Working paper no.43.

Nellis (2005) Privatization in Africa: What has happened? What is to be done? Fondazione Enrico Mattei, Nota di Lavoro 127, Milan, Italy.

The New York Times (2014) 'In Nigeria, Chinese investment comes with a downside', Online: http://www.nytimes.com/2015/12/06/business/international/in-nigeria-chinese-investment-comes-with-a-downside.html?_r=0 (accessed 19 January 2016).

North, D. (1993) 'The new institutional economics & development', Working Paper, Ronald Coase Institute. Online: http://www2.econ.iastate.edu/testatsi/NewTaste.north.pdf.

OECD (nd) *Africa Fact Sheet: Main Economic Indicators*, Paris: OECD.

Oyugi, W. (1994) 'Kenya: contextual factors & the policy process', in Picard, L. & Garrity, M. (eds.) *Policy Reform for Sustainable Development in Africa*, Boulder: Lynne Rienner.

Ozawa, T. (2016) *The Evolution of the World Economy: The "Flying-Geese" Theory of Multinational Corporations & Structural Transformation*, Cheltenham, UK & Northampton, MA: Elgar.

Ozawa, T. (2015) 'Next great industrial transmigration: relocating China's factories to Sub-Saharan Africa, Flying-Geese style', Asia-Pacific Economic Cooperation, Columbia University, Discussion paper, no. 78. Online: https://www8.gsb.columbia.edu/apec/sites/apec/files/DP%2078.Ozawa_.China%20in%20Africa.pdf.

Pack, H. (1982) 'Aggregate implications of factor substitution in industrial processes', *Journal of Development Economics*, 11,1:1–38.

Pack, H. (1981) 'Fostering the capital goods sector in developing countries', *World Development*, 9,3:227–250.

Page, J. (2012) 'Can Africa industrialise?', *Journal of African Economies*, 21:86–125.

Palmade, V. Chandra, V. & H. Dinh (2010) 'China's secret weapon in light manufacturing: small & medium enterprise-oriented "plug & play" industrial zones', World Bank blog. Online: http://blogs.worldbank.org/developmenttalk/chinas-secret-weapon-in-light-manufacturing-small-and-medium-enterprise-oriented-plug-and-play-indus (accessed 27 March 2014).

Pew Research Center (2015) 'Sub-Saharan Africa makes rogress against poverty but has long way to go', Washington, DC.

Phillips, D. (1979) 'Industrialization in Tanzania,' in Kim, K. Mabele, R. & Schultheis, M. (eds.) *Papers on the Political Economy of Tanzania*, Nairobi: Heinemann.

Picard, L. (1994) 'The challenge of structural adjustment', in Picard, L. & Garrity, M. (eds.) *Policy Reform for Sustainable Development in Africa*, Boulder: Lynne Rienner.

Pietrobelli, C. (2006) 'Fostering technological capabilities in Sub-Saharan Africa', Science & Development Network. Online: http://www.scidev.net/en/policy-briefs (accessed 4 October 2012).

Pigato, M. & Tang, W. (2015) 'China & Africa: Expanding Economic Ties in an Evolving Global Context', Investing in Africa Forum, Addis Ababa, The World Bank.

Pigato, M. & Gourdon, J. (2014) 'The impact of rising Chinese trade & development assistance in West Africa', Africa trade practice working paper series no. 4, Washington, D.C.: World Bank Group. Online: http://documents.worldbank.org/curated/en/2014/05/1rising-Chinese-trade-and-development-assistance-in-West-Africa (accessed 1 March 2015)

Podeh, E. & Winckler, O. (2004) *Rethinking Nasserism: Revolution & Historical Memory in Modern Egypt*, Gainsville: University of Florida Press.

Prahalad, C.K. (2004) *The Fortune at the Bottom of the Pyramid*, Philadelphia: Wharton School Publishing.

Ranis, G. (1973) 'Industrial sector labor absorption', *Economic Development & Cultural Change*, 21, 3:387–408.

Ranis, G. & Saxonhouse, G. (1983) 'International & domestic determinants of technology choice by the less developed countries', in Lucas, B. & Freedman, S. (eds.) *Technology Choice & Change in Developing Countries: Internal & External Constraints*, Dublin: Tycooly International.

Ray, D. (1998) *Development Economics*, Princeton, NJ: Princeton University Press.

Reddy, P. (1997) 'New trends in globalization of corporate R&D and implications for innovation capability in host countries: a survey from India', *World Development*, 25, 11:1821–1837.

Research ICT Africa (2011) 'Household, small business & public institutional e-access & usage survey 2011', Cape Town: South Africa.

Rodrik, D. (2015) 'Premature deindustrialization', NBER, working paper no. 20935.

Rodrik, D. (2014) 'An African growth miracle?', NBER, working paper 20188.

Rodrik, D. (2013) 'The past, present, & future of economic growth', Institute of Advanced Study, Princeton University, online: https://www.sss.ias.edu/files/pdfs/Rodrik/Research/Structural-Change-Fundamentals-and-Growth-An-Overview_revised.pdf (accessed 30 July 2015).

Roemer, M., Tidrick, G. & Williams, D. (1976) 'The range of strategic choice in Tanzanian industry', *Journal of Development Economics*, 3:257–275.

Ross, M. (1999) 'The political economy of the resource curse', *World Politics*, 51:297–322.

SciDevNet (2015) 'Focus on private sector: India's generic drug wars', online: http://www.scidev.net/global/medicine/analysis-blog/private-sector-india-generic-drug-wars.html (accessed 11 August 2015).

Seers, D. (1962) 'The limitations of the Special Case', *Bulletin of the Oxford Institute of Economics & Statistics*, 25,2:77–98.

Sen, A. (1985) *Commodities & Capabilities*, Amsterdam: North-Holland.

Shakya, M. (2011) 'Apparel exports in Lesotho: The state's role in building critical mass for competitiveness. In P. Chuhan-Pole and M. Angwafo (eds.) *Yes Africa Can Success Stories from a Dynamic Continent*. Washington, DC: The International Bank for Reconstruction and Development/The World Bank.

Shen, X. (2015) 'Private Chinese investment in Africa: myths & realities', *Development Policy Review*, 33,1:83–106.

Silberschmidt, M. (2001) 'Disempowerment of men in rural and urban East Africa: implications for male identity and sexual behavior,' *World Development*, 29, 4:657–671.

Silverman, J. (1992) 'Public sector decentralization', World Bank Technical Paper no. 188, Washington, D.C.

Solow, R. (1990) *The Labour Market as a Social Institution*, Oxford: Blackwell.

Solow, R. (1956) 'A contribution to the theory of economic growth', *Quarterly Journal of Economics*, 70,1:65–94.

Stewart, F. (2010) 'Horizontal inequalities in Kenya & the political disturbances of 2008: some implications for aid policy', *Conflict, Security & Development*, 10,1:133–159.

Stewart, F. (ed) (1987) *Macro-Policies for Appropriate Technology*, Boulder, CO: Westview.

Stewart, F. (1977) *Technology & Underdevelopment*, London: Macmillan.

Stewart, F., Lall, S. & Wangwe, S. (eds.) (1992) *Alternative Development Strategies in Sub-Saharan Africa*, London: Macmillan.

Stock, E. & de Veen, J. (1996) 'Expanding labour-based methods for road works in Africa', World Bank Technical paper no. 347, Washington, D.C, D.C.

Sun, Y. (2015) 'China's foreign aid reform & implications for Africa', Brookings Institution. Online: https://www.brookings.edu/blog/africa-in-focus/2015/07/01/chinas-foreign-aid-reform-and-implications-for-africa/ (accessed 29 March 2015).

Sun, Y. (2014) 'China's aid to Africa: Monster or Messiah?' Brookings, East Asian Commentary, online: https://www.brookings.edu/opinions/chinas-aid-to-africa-monster-or-messiah/ (accessed 19 March 2015).

Timss (2011) *Trends in International Mathematics & Science Study*, Boston: Boston College. Online: http://timss.bc.edu/timss2011/index.html (accessed 26 July, 2016)

Todaro, M. & Smith, S. (2011) *Economic Development*, 11th edn. Harlow: Pearson.

Tregenna, F. (2012) 'Sectoral labour-intensity in South Africa', NEDLAC Labour Intensity Report, online: http://new.nedlac.org.za/wp-content/uploads/2014/10/labour_intensity_report_2010.pdf (accessed 12 February, 2016).

UN (2015) World population prospects: the 2015 revision, New York: United Nations. Online: http://esa.un.org/undp/wpp/publications/files/key (accessed 10 February 2016).

UNDP (2001) *Human Development Report: Making New Technologies Work for Human Development*, New York: Oxford University Press.

UNECA (2014) Dynamic Industrial Policy in Africa, Economic report on Africa. Online: http://www.uneca.org/sites/default/files/PublicationFiles/final_era2014_march25_en.pdf. (accessed 3 April 2015).

UNIDO & UNCTAD (2011) *The Economic Development of Africa Report*, Vienna and Geneva: United Nations.

UNIDO (2013) *Industrial Development Report*, Vienna: UNIDO.

UNIDO (2011) *Economic Development of Africa Report*, Vienna: UNIDO.

UNODC (2011) *Global study on Homicide*, Vienna: United Nations Office on Drugs and Crime.

van Kempen, L. (2005) *Status Competition and Poverty in Developing Countries*, unpublished Ph.D dissertation, CentER, Tilburg University, The Netherlands.

Vastveit, L. (2013) 'Export processing zones in Sub-Saharan Africa – Kenya & Lesotho', Department of Economics, University of Bremen. Online: http://bora.uib.no/bitstream/handle/1956/7611/115918722.pdf?sequence=1.

Von Tunzelmann, N. (1981) 'Technical progress during the industrial revolution', in Floud, R. & Mcloskey, D. (eds.) *The Economic History of Britain since 1700, Vol. 1, 1700–1860* Cambridge: Cambridge University Press.

Wangwe, S. (1992) 'Building indigenous technological capacity in African industry', in Stewart, F., Lall, S. & Wangwe, S. (eds.) *Alternative Development Strategies in Sub-Saharan Africa*, London: Macmillan.

Waning, B., Diedrichsen, E. and Moon, S. (2010) "A lifeline to treatment: the role of Indian generic manufacturers in supplying antiretroviral medicines to developing countries", *Journal of AIDS Society*, September 14: 13–35.

World Bank (2015a) *Manufacturing FDI in Sub-Saharan Africa*, Washington, D.C.

World Bank (2015b) *Global Economic Prospects*, Washington, D.C.

World Bank (2015c) *FDI and Manufacturing in Africa*, online: http://www.worldbank.org/content/dam/Worldbank/Event/Africa/Investing%20in%20Africa%20Forum/2015/investing-in-africa-forum-fdi-and-manufacturing-in-africa.pdf. Accessed 4 February, 2016).

World Bank (2015d) *Transforming Ethiopia into a Manufacturing Powerhouse Requires Skills Development and Improved Investment Climate*. Online: https://www.google.nl#q=world+bank+ethiopia+2015+industrial+parks (accessed 30 April 2015).

World Bank (2013a) *African Competitiveness Report*, Washington, D.C.

World Bank (2013b) *Africa's Pulse*, October, 8.

World Bank (2011) *World Development Report*, Washington, D.C.

World Bank (2012) *World Development Report 2013*, New York: Oxford University Press.

World Bank (1999) *Madagascar – Pilot Regional Project*, The Infoshop, Washington, D.C

World Bank (1995) *Bureaucrats in Business*, Oxford: Oxford University Press.

Index

For Product Safety Concerns and Information please contact our EU
representative GPSR@taylorandfrancis.com
Taylor & Francis Verlag GmbH, Kaufingerstraße 24, 80331 München, Germany

www.ingramcontent.com/pod-product-compliance
Ingram Content Group UK Ltd.
Pitfield, Milton Keynes, MK11 3LW, UK
UKHW020948180425
457613UK00019B/594